HELP for the LAID OFF

Mary Aucoin Kaarto

Bridge-Logos
Alachua, Florida 32615

Bridge-Logos
Alachua, FL 32615 USA

Help for the Laid Off
by Mary Aucoin Kaarto

Copyright ©2009 by Bridge-Logos

All rights reserved. Under International Copyright Law, no part of this publication may be reproduced, stored, or transmitted by any means—electronic, mechanical, photographic (photocopy), recording, or otherwise—without written permission from the Publisher.

Printed in the United States of America.

Library of Congress Catalog Card Number: 2009926924
International Standard Book Number 978-0-88270-989-5

Scripture quotations in this book are from the *King James Version* of the Bible.

Unless otherwise indicated, Scripture quotations are taken from the *New American Standard Bible*. © 1960, 1962, 1963, 1968, 1971, 1972, 1973, 1975, 1977 by The Lockman Foundation. Used by permission.

Scripture quotations marked NIV are taken from the *Holy Bible, New International Version®*. NIV®. Copyright © 1973, 1978, 1984 by International Bible Society. Used by permission of Zondervan. All rights reserved.

Scripture quotations marked NLT are taken from the *Holy Bible, New Living Translation,* copyright © 1996. Used by permission of Tyndale House Publishers, Inc., Wheaton, Illinois 60189. All rights reserved.

Scripture quotations marked NKJV taken from the *New King James Version.* Copyright © 1979, 1980, 1982 by Thomas Nelson, Inc. Used by permission. All rights reserved.

Back cover author photo by Robert Eisenmann.

G616.316.N.m905.35230

Contents

Acknowledgements ix

Introduction xiii

1 Trusting God in a Layoff. 1

2 Creating Sanity in a New Reality 21

3 Your Job is to Find a Job 37

4 Spending Your Spare Time 49

5 Money Matters 61

6 Lessons Learned from Layoff 101 75

7 Layoffs Produce an Abundance of Fruitful
   Blessings 93

8 Encourage Your Discouraged 105

9 You're in the Promised Land—Now What? 123

10 U.S. Pastors Speak Out on How Layoffs
    Affect the Church 129

Epilogue 141

This book is dedicated to God, Emilie, and the millions of hurting people who are between jobs and living from minute to minute.
I am with you, my friends.

Acknowledgements

The writing of this book would not have been possible without the privilege of being allowed to undergo a layoff experience not once, but twice. Thank you, Lord, for loving me enough to put me through my own "Job experiences." All glory, honor, and praise belong to you, the true author of this book.

A special thank-you goes to Emilie McDonald for being the best daughter in the world. Thank you for your sweetness and generosity in treating me to movies when I couldn't afford them, for giving me a little extra money from your paychecks when you weren't paying your own way. May you always follow the advice found in Proverbs 3:5-6.

Thank you to my family for loving and supporting Emilie and me during this current and previous layoff. A special thank-you to my brother, Pat Aucoin, for being "the man of the family" for the thirty-plus years since Daddy died. I also thank God for my sisters—Pam Lippold, Linda Eisenmann, and Anne Hill—for their love and companionship throughout the years. Thank you to my sister-in-law, Martha Aucoin, and my brother-in-law, Lee Hill, for being willing to share your families' incomes when I needed it. May I never take the generosity of others for granted.

My church family at Second Baptist Church ("Second") has shown me the love of Christ from the day I joined in 1999. An enormous thank-you to Dr. Ed Young, senior pastor, for loving us all enough to share the whole truth about God and His Word in such fresh and exciting ways. God has spoken to me through your teaching more than you could ever know. Thank you.

To Dr. James DeLoach, thank you for loving me enough to call me "daughter." After more than thirty years without a dad, I have informally adopted you! Your time, wisdom, patience, and prayers have helped my walk with the Lord more than you'll ever know. I will never forget my time with you and Doris.

Dr. Wallace Henley, thank you for your advice during this layoff and for helping me navigate my way through the gauntlet of pain my family and I went through, watching our mother suffer and die.

To Karen Zurawski and Oliver Klinger, thank you for making my dreams of writing for a living come true. You cannot know how much I appreciated these opportunities.

Among the sweet bouquet of friends God has blessed me with, who have helped me throughout this layoff and whose relationships mean everything to me, are Tory Cammeresi, Cathy Burge, Stella Zepeda, Sherri Tschirhart, and Deb Whittier.

I also give thanks to my parents, Patrick and Janice, whom I miss so much.

Last but not least, I am thankful for John, my husband and best friend. Thank you for the unconditional love, indescribable joy, and support you give me. There is no one I would rather share my life with than you.

Acknowledgements

There are so many people in my life who have helped me through these two layoffs. It is my most sincere hope that I have not forgotten anyone. If I have, please forgive me, as it was not intentional.

Thank you, Tiffany Morgan, my editor, Shawn Myers, my publicist, and Peggy Hildebrand, acquisitions editor at Bridge-Logos, for giving me the chance to help those who are laid off and hurting.

Although I've never had the pleasure of meeting the following individuals, I want to thank them for their ministries, all of which I have enjoyed listening to and have been helped by: Charles Stanley, *In Touch Ministries* (www.intouch.org); Pastor James McDonald, *Walk in the Word* (www.walkintheword.com); Dave Ramsey, *The Dave Ramsey Show* (www.daveramsey.com); and Joyce Meyer, *Enjoying Everyday Life* (www.joycemeyer.org).

Introduction

Being confident of this, that He who began a good work in you will carry it on to completion until the day of Christ Jesus.
Philippians 1:6

Millions of people are affected by layoffs, not just those whose jobs have been eliminated. Let me explain.

Get a sheet of paper and draw yourself in the middle. Obviously, you, as the layoff victim, are affected most of all. Now, draw a circle around yourself and within it, the names of your spouse and/or children. Their lives are altered because suddenly the possibility of losing their home, cars, the ability to participate in after-school activities, or go to the beauty shop becomes very real.

Next, draw a larger circle, and inside of it write the names of your parents, brothers, and sisters. Though not hit quite as hard, your immediate family is affected nonetheless, if they are sending money as often as they are able and are supporting you on emotional, physical, and spiritual levels. Helping to support you with part of their income takes away from their families, but you are *not* to feel guilty about this. Nine chances out of ten, you—like me—did nothing to cause the loss of your job.

The same thing that happened to us can happen to them tomorrow morning.

Draw a third circle to represent your circle of friends, who, if you're blessed with good friends as I am, will stick with you as thick as thieves.

Finally, draw a fourth circle to represent the Body of Christ, our church families as a whole. Benevolence funds are more quickly depleted each month due to the increase in families needing assistance due to layoffs, as are the amount of tithes and offerings. Read more on this in Chapter Ten.

In 2003, there were as many as 9.3 million people claiming unemployment benefits at one time in America, not to mention the millions who had already exhausted their benefits but yet are still without work. Perhaps —like me—you are one of them. In fact, as I write this book, I am smack-dab in the middle of another layoff. Please bear with me, while I briefly share my testimony.

As a single mom, I came to know and trust the Lord during my first layoff, which began in 1994. I was emotionally flat-lined when I first heard the news, because I did *not* see it coming. When the layoff ended two years later in 1996, not only was I blessed with the career change I'd only dreamed of having, but I also have been able ever since to witness to many people who have lost their jobs and all hope for a brighter future. I learned that God loved me and would always take care of me, but the only way I came to that conclusion was to first experience the need for Him, and then to turn to and trust Him.

My reaction to this current layoff, which occurred on October 31, 2002, was radically different to the one

Introduction

I had in 1994. Trick or treat. *Not!* "Oh, really? That's okay. It just means the Lord has something better for me to do." God knew how much I enjoyed my last job, and because of it, He knew that I would never willingly leave the company on my own. In order for Him to place me in line to receive a better opportunity and blessings, God allowed and possibly even created this layoff in order for me to do so.

Two weeks after I was laid off, I was trying to save money by pruning my twenty-five-year old oak tree in the backyard. In the process, I fell 16 feet off my ladder, *Charlie's Angels* style (hands and feet flat to the ground). A single, laid-off mom has to do what a single, laid-off mom has to do! As a result of that brilliant move, I broke my right leg, tore the meniscus in the same leg, and injured my right arm. For almost a year, I hobbled around on crutches and used a walker and a cane, trying to pretend there wasn't something seriously wrong with my knee. When you don't have a job, and you don't have money, and you don't have medical insurance, you just stand through the pain for as long as possible. Pun intended. Undoubtedly the worst event I've experienced during this current layoff was losing my mother unexpectedly due to medical negligence within days of my having knee surgery.

God allowed or possibly even created these sanctified experiences to make me housebound and give me the time to do what He has called me to do: write this book about trusting Him through a layoff. I am humbled and grateful that He would use someone like me for your good and His glory!

My friend, there is *no telling* what God is up to in your life or why He allowed this layoff for you. But if you respond to this adversity the right way—by turning to and trusting Him—you are in for the adventure of a lifetime and one in which you will be richly blessed.

Using God's wisdom and guidance through many passages of Scripture, the purpose of this book is to teach you how to live fully, joyfully, obediently, and expectantly. If you respond to this crisis by reaching out to God, one day you will look back on this period in your life and be grateful for it. You will be able to see God's hand all over the place, working through the lives of other believers to minister to and provide for you. You and others in your life will learn many important lessons, and you will be in line to receive blessings too numerous to count when your layoff is over. More importantly, you will be equipped to minister to others whom God will place in your path at some point in the future.

> *Praise be to the God and Father of our Lord Jesus Christ, the Father of compassion and the God of all comfort, who comforts us in all our troubles, so that we can comfort those in any trouble with the comfort we ourselves have received from God. (2 Corinthians 1:3-4)*

However, if you do not allow yourself to be humbled by God and learn to trust Him, there is a good chance you will have suffered for nothing. You see, God has great plans for your life, and He allows us hard times to draw closer to Him and get to know Him better. It is one thing to know about God, but it is an entirely different thing to *know* Him. The best way to get to know God is to let Him reveal to you one step at a time His awesome, mighty love for you. Please don't be like the Israelites in the Old Testament, taking forty years to complete a journey that should have lasted eleven days!

Hope Springs Eternal

The good news is that you—like me—are going to be okay. Everything is going to be fine. Despite how you may be feeling at this moment, being laid off is an incredible gift and blessing from the Lord that you do *not* want to miss. As Christians, God is our Divine Employer. Reading His Word and being obedient to His commands will not only see us through these layoffs, but also will help us to walk out of the fire in a whole new light with a keen sense of purpose and direction for our lives.

Calm down, breathe deeply, and whatever you do, take heart and know that there is joyful life to be lived during—and in spite of—being without work. Understand in your heart of hearts that God will lead you and me out of this desert one day, after His purposes for us have been fulfilled. You will find gainful employment, and so will I.

> *For the Lord your God is bringing you into a good land—a land with streams and pools of water, with springs flowing in the valleys and hills. (Deuteronomy 8:7)*

The Lord is my real boss, and I shall not want.
He gives me peace, when chaos is all around me.
He gently reminds me to pray before I speak, and
To do all things without murmuring or complaining.
He reminds me that He is my source and not my job.
He restores my sanity every day and guides my decisions, that
I might honor Him in everything I do.
Even though I face absurd amounts of email, system crashes,
Unrealistic deadlines, budget cutbacks, gossiping co-workers,
Discriminating supervisors and an aging body that doesn't cooperate every morning,
I will not stop—for He is with me!
His presence, His peace and His power will see me through.
He raises me up even when they fail to promote me.
He claims me for His own, even when the company threatens to let me go.
His faithfulness and love are better than any bonus check, and
His retirement plan beats every 401K there is!
When it is all said and done, I'll be working for Him a whole lot
Longer and for that, I bless His name.

—Anonymous

Chapter One

Trusting God in a Layoff

Welcome to Layoff 101—your new, albeit temporary, reality.

I know how *you* feel, but I want you to know how *I* feel: excited and hopeful about your future and mine. Based on my first layoff experience and this present one, I can tell you with full confidence and assurance that God is a trustworthy, compassionate, and faithful Father who loves you, and *all* of His promises found in the Bible are true. If you do not believe any of this today, you will by the time your layoff has ended.

In Chapter One, I will strive to explain what God *may* be doing in your life behind the scenes and why He *may* have allowed or even created this experience for you to endure. I want to help you accept the unacceptable because until you do, you will be unable to learn how to respond to a layoff in a way that is pleasing to God. Once you understand and learn the steps contained in this book, He will show you so many amazing things about Him and yourself. God will reveal His purposes for you during your layoff, and after He helps you accomplish them, He will walk you directly to your own Promised Land! So, work with me here!

What's Happening?

Years ago, there was a popular film called *Poltergeist*. During one segment in the film, a young teenage girl is scared and confused about the strange goings-on in her home. "What's happening?!" she screams. Have you felt this way? I know I did during my first layoff.

It is normal and natural to wonder why you lost your job. Was it something you said or did not say, did or did not do? Is it because of the anemic economy resulting since September 11, 2001, or corporate greed?

Perhaps God has purposely enrolled you in Layoff 101 to test your faith or remind you that you are completely dependent upon Him for everything. Maybe it's for both reasons. Moses reminds us of this in Deuteronomy 8:2-3. Check it out:

> *Remember how the Lord your God led you all the way in the desert these forty years, to humble you and to test you in order to know what was in your heart, whether or not you would keep His commands. He humbled you, causing you to hunger and then feeding you manna, which neither you nor your fathers had known, to teach you that man does not live on bread alone but on every word that comes out of the mouth of the Lord.*

Ask yourself if this layoff is a form of discipline or protection from the Lord. Did you take your regular source of income for granted, buy a lot of toys you didn't need, and hike up your credit-card debt in the process? Perhaps you swiped a few office supplies or used the postage machine for personal mail. Solomon writes in Proverbs 20:17, "Bread obtained by falsehood tastes sweet to a man, but afterward his mouth will be filled with gravel." Maybe you were surfing the Internet on company time, and they decided to wave you goodbye. The company is paying you to work, after all.

Could it be that you were bored with your job, and as such, became lazy and didn't do it at all or to the best of your ability? "Lazy hands make a man poor, but diligent hands bring wealth" (Proverbs 10:4).

Please don't misunderstand me here. I'm not accusing you or anyone else of doing anything wrong, nor am I saying that everyone who is laid off deserves it. But I would not be serving you well if I did not at least offer these ideas up for your consideration.

Know then in your heart that as a man disciplines his son, so the Lord your God disciplines you. (Deuteronomy 8:5)

Whoever loves discipline loves knowledge, but he who hates correction is stupid. (Proverbs 12:1)

Was there someone of the opposite sex at your former place of employment whose presence you were tempted by? I don't have to tell you how much God and your spouse value the marriage covenant, do I? And if you are single, need I remind you that sex outside of marriage goes directly against God's plan for your life? Praise God for getting you out of that situation before you were tempted to cheat on your spouse or have sex outside of marriage!

It could be that even though you are the one who was laid off, this situation may not be about you at all, but a test for those *around* you. Perhaps God is testing the faith and obedience of your family members and friends. Are they going to step up to the plate and support you on every level possible or let you sink into despair? Are your family and friends going to pass judgment on you and wrongly assume or accuse you of wrongdoing, or are they going to be filled with compassion toward you? Maybe you are estranged from someone you love, and God has brought this layoff into your life as a means of reconciliation.

Could it be that God knows you were miserable in your last position, but up until now you have been afraid to try something new by following your own "yellow-brick road" to the career path you've always dreamed? Perhaps God created this layoff as a way of "strongly encouraging" you to go for it? Check *this* promise out!

> *For I know the plans I have for you, declares the LORD, plans to prosper you and not to harm you, plans to give you hope and a future. Then you will call upon me and come and pray to me, and I will listen to you. (Jeremiah 29:11-12)*

Maybe your marriage needed strengthening, your children needed to learn the value of a dollar the hard way, or your last job was giving you health problems that could have progressed into something more serious, had you kept it.

Whatever the reasons for this layoff, I wouldn't waste too much time pondering "why," but more time asking, "God, what are you trying to teach me through this?"

Basic Training

Maybe God is sifting and strengthening you for future service.

Let me ask you something: Who are you going to go to for advice for any given circumstance? Someone who has been through it or someone who has not? Surely you would prefer to talk with someone who knows what you're going through. Eight years after my first layoff ended, I learned that God allowed that first experience (and even this current one) to help you by writing this book. Like me, one day your layoff will end, you will graduate from Layoff 101, and you will be able to, with full conviction, help others who God will intentionally place in your path. Your pain and suffering will not have been in vain! One of the biggest gifts you will receive is the joy of helping others in your future.

> *See, I will make you into a threshing sledge, new and sharp, with many teeth. You will thresh the mountains and crush them, and reduce the hills to chaff. You will winnow them, the wind will pick them up, and a gale will blew them away. But you will rejoice in the Lord and glory in the Holy One of Israel. (Isaiah 41:15-16)*

In his letter to Timothy, the Apostle Paul explains what we must do to be used by God. "In a large house there are articles not only of gold and silver, but also of wood and clay; some are for noble purposes and some for ignoble. If a man cleanses himself from the latter, he will be an instrument for noble purposes, made holy, useful to the Master and prepared to do any good work" (2 Timothy 2:20-21).

Sifting shakes us up, helps cleanse us from our sin, and is a form of spiritual surgery on our souls. Even though it hurts, I recommend embracing the process and letting God's will be done. The sooner you cooperate with the changes God wants to make in you, the sooner you will be taken out of the fire! He also knows what He wants to do with you, and He's not going to change His mind about you. So, you might as well go with God's program and enjoy His blessings!

> *Oh people of Zion, who live in Jerusalem, you will weep no more. How gracious He will be when you cry for help! As soon as He hears, He will answer you. Although the Lord gives you the bread of adversity and the water of affliction, your teachers will be hidden no more; with your own eyes you will see them. Whether you turn to the right or to the left, your ears will hear a voice behind you, saying, "This is the way; walk in it." (Isaiah 30:19-21)*

> *For men are not cast off by the Lord forever. Though He brings grief, He will show compassion, so great is His unfailing love. (Lamentations 3:31-32)*

Perhaps you were wrongly accused of something, or were someone's scapegoat. If this is the case, take comfort in knowing that the same God who provided for Hagar in the Old Testament is going to provide for you. But don't take my word for it—let's look at what happened in the book of Genesis.

Booted, Then Blessed

Abram and his wife, Sarai, had grown very old and were without children. In those days, people looked down upon you if you had no children of your own. God promised Abram that a son from his "own body" would become his heir (Genesis 15:4). Not only did God tell him this, but He took Abram outside and also told him that his offspring would be more in number than the stars in the sky. While Abram believed God, and it was credited to him as righteousness, Sarai did not.

Sarai became impatient and, after ten years of waiting, decided Abram should have sex with her maidservant, Hagar, in hopes that Hagar would become pregnant and give Sarai the child to bring up as her own. She became jealous of Hagar after her plan worked, and little Ishmael was born. Sarai then gave Abram an ultimatum: her or me. Abram told Sarai to do whatever she wanted with Hagar, thus giving his wife permission to be abusive to the maidservant until she left them. (See Genesis 16:6.)

The angel of the Lord found Hagar near a spring in the desert, and asked what she was doing there. "Then the angel of the Lord told her, 'Go back to your mistress and submit to her.' The angel added, 'I will so increase your descendants that they will be too numerous to count'" (Genesis 16:9-10).

Although God promised Abram and Sarai a child of their own, Abram loved Ishmael and asked God to take care of him. God told Abraham (formerly Abram), "And as for Ishmael, I have heard you: I will surely bless him; I will make him fruitful and will greatly increase his numbers. He will be the father of twelve rulers, and I will make him into a great nation" (Genesis 17:20).

Even though Hagar was used, abused and for all intended purposes, run off from her job, God restored her and made sure that she and Ishmael not only survived, but also thrived. My friend, God always restores the righteous and makes sure that justice is served in His perfect time and in His perfect way. And, He will take care of you and your family, as He took care of Hagar and Ishmael.

Do not say, "I'll pay you back for this wrong!" Wait for the Lord, and He will deliver you. (Proverbs 20:22)

Feel Your Feelings

Shock, anger and disbelief are all normal emotions during a layoff. Losing your job, especially if you are the sole provider and/or a single parent, is one of the most stressful experiences anyone could ever endure.

One of the best things you can do for yourself is beginning to journal your thoughts and feelings online, in a Word document, spiral notebook, or journal. You can express yourself to yourself, and it is a very therapeutic experience. I would also recommend beginning a separate prayer journal. In a new Word document or in a notebook of some type, make two columns per page.

On one side, list your prayer request and date. I usually find an appropriate Scripture verse to accompany the specific prayer request and include it at the end. The right column is where you'll write God's answer to each prayer, along with the date. For so many years this practice was recommended to me, and I thought it was silly. That was, until I started doing it. The reason it is so beneficial is because on days when your faith is non-existent or running dry, you can flip through the pages of this journal and see written documentation of how God is faithful to answer your prayers, every time.

There is a definitive grieving process that most people go through after losing their job, and it is similar to that of someone who has lost a loved one, according to Katherine Moore, of Christian Counseling Associates. "The stages of grief are denial, anger, bargaining, depression/despair and resolution. It doesn't necessarily happen in a smooth curve and it doesn't happen necessarily in that order," she said. Following is an explanation of the grieving process, according to Moore.

Denial is about facing the impact of the loss; for example, not really looking at what has been lost in completeness, the losses, and the effect on life, lives, the future, permanent changes, and the efforts to move on.

Anger is about the loss of control but is also projected onto whom or what is gone; for example, the person who is deceased or the job that is left behind, the people and/or the organization, etc. Anger can also be integrated into denial, especially when it is easier to be angry than to face the reality of the situation, because that means giving up control of the situation. Anger can also get immersed into the bargaining stage, because once bargaining fails, anger comes out—this time, mostly at God.

Bargaining has to do mostly with illnesses or job loss and not so much with death. It is the attitude that "Maybe I can fix it, look for a cure, or find a great job right away because I will do all the right things when looking for work."

Despair/Hopelessness come into play after the reality sets in that you are no longer in control of your situation. That is the big thing then, dealing with the losses, the lack of control over circumstances. Loneliness, isolation, and a "just God and me" type of thinking come into play during this stage. Cry if you need to. By the way, did you know God saves your tears in a jar? It's true.

Resolution surfaces after reality is allowed to sink in, coping skills are revitalized in a new way, one's perspective changes, and the future is contemplated, melding loss with the process of moving on.

When you become depressed—and you will—the quickest way out is to praise God through prayers and songs. I know, I know. It doesn't make sense, and I doubted this method too when I first heard it. But I did it anyway, and guess what? It really, really worked.

Another way to claim victory over depression is to boldly take the authority over Satan that Jesus gave you.

> *I have given you authority to trample on snakes and scorpions and to overcome all the power of the enemy; nothing will harm you. (Luke 10:19)*

If you are angry with God, tell Him. If you are scared, tell Him. Our Father will not leave you, nor will

He forsake you. Don't allow your emotions to rule over you, especially when making decisions that will affect your life and the lives of your family. Worrying is not just a waste of time, but Jesus specifically commands us over and over again not to do it because it shows a lack of faith and trust in God.

If you are living in regret over things you've said or done in the past—or worrying about tomorrow—Satan will have succeeded at stealing your today. In fact, when Satan sees the many blessings God has in store for you and for me, he will do whatever it takes to get us to dwell on past mistakes to conjure up fear and doubt so we will not move forward in obedience to God and understand His purposes for our pain.

The Apostle Paul, beaten and imprisoned for sharing the gospel, was someone who understood the concept of the past being the past and the pointlessness of worrying. He writes:

> *Brothers, I do not consider myself yet to have taken hold of it. But one thing I do: Forgetting what is behind and straining toward what is ahead, I press on toward the goal to win the prize for which God has called me heavenward in Christ Jesus. (Philippians 3:13-14)*

Paul's remedy for worrying was to change his way of thinking. Think of things that are true, noble, right, pure, lovely, and admirable; if anything is excellent or praiseworthy, think about those things (Philippians 4:8).

Do not wallow in your grief for too long, do not have a pity party and do not give up and become lazy. The sooner you bounce back, the better your chances are of finding gainful employment.

> *The sluggard craves and gets nothing, but the desires of the diligent are fully satisfied. (Proverbs 13:4)*

When you become afraid—and you will—you are giving Satan entry into every corner of your life. Remember that fear is Satan's antidote to faith. He hates you and your loved ones, and there is nothing he would rather do than use this layoff experience to bring you down, destroy your marriage, harm your children by taking their innocence too soon, and most damaging of all—try to snatch you out of God's lap (even though this is impossible, if you are a believer). The closer you are to God, the more Satan is going to attack. Submit to God, resist the devil and he will flee!

So, give yourself a week—two at the most—to work through your feelings, and then make a conscious decision to get over it. All things come to an end. Remember that endings are not endings—they are beginnings just being born. Pity and pride don't pay the bills. You have work to do!

> *Forget the former things; do not dwell on the past. See, I am doing a new thing! Now it springs up; do you not perceive it? I am making a way in the desert and streams in the wasteland. (Isaiah 43:18)*

Growing and Learning Through Adversity

Everyone experiences painful trials by fire and adversity throughout life because God does not want us to be self-sufficient. He wants us to depend on Him for everything. To accomplish this, God places us in situations where we are forced to recognize and admit our need for Him, so that He can reveal himself to us in ways that are nothing short of amazing. God calls us unto himself so that we can become effective witnesses of His grace, love, mercy, protection, and provision.

Oftentimes, how long we remain in the valley depends on how well we behave while we're in it. The Apostle Paul wrote in Acts 14:22, "… strengthening the disciples and encouraging them to remain true to the faith. 'We must go through many hardships to enter the kingdom of God …'" Think of it this way: No matter what we go through in this life, nothing compares to the pain and suffering Christ went through on our undeserving behalf. Nothing. You know it, and I know it.

Once we have learned these truths for ourselves through enduring our layoff experiences, God will provide us with a new way to earn a living. We will then be given the opportunity to go out into the world and share what we have learned with others who may not know Him.

When all these blessings and curses I have set before you come upon you and you take them to heart wherever the Lord your God disperses you among the nations, and when you and your children return to the Lord your God and obey him with all your heart and with all your soul

> *according to everything I command you today, then the Lord your God will restore your fortunes and have compassion on you and gather you again from all the nations where He scattered you. (Deuteronomy 30:1-3)*

Listen, in case you haven't noticed, life on Earth is not exactly nirvana! No one said life would ever be easy. In fact, "Life is difficult," as M. Scott Peck, M.D., points out in the opening lines of his runaway bestseller, *The Road Less Traveled*. Many pastors have taught that God is not nearly as interested in our pleasure and enjoyment as He is in developing character. If we were able to reverse history and live on Earth as Adam and Eve did before the fall of mankind, now *that* would be the proverbial "Heaven on Earth"!

Rest assured that God never leaves us or forsakes us, especially during trials. When you feel fearful about what God is calling you to do, well, do it afraid! What do you think I'm feeling as I write this book—courage or fear? Big clue: *fear!* I'm no great spiritual giant; I'm just a regular non-working stiff like you, who happens to really love God.

You Have a Bright Future—Really!

Now don't blow a gasket when I tell you this: There will come a day and time when all you are feeling will be gone, you *will* have a new job, and better yet—you will look back on this time of your life and thank God for every miserable moment of it. I want you to get *excited* over the fact that God loves you enough to allow or even cause this layoff as a way of drawing you closer to Him.

Perhaps you have known "about God" all your life, but you don't really know Him and because of that, you're terrified of the darkness you find yourself in. You don't recognize your surroundings, you don't understand why you lost your job, nor do you know what lies ahead. And worst of all, your ability to "fly the plane" has been taken from you. Are you going to let this layoff result in a crashing experience or a soaring one?

God's divine will for your life was to pick you up from where you were and put you down on a new road, one that will allow you to get to know *Him* on a personal level. Think about it. How else do you get to know someone and develop a friendship? You spend time together, you talk and you listen. If there was ever a time when you needed to talk to and listen to God, it is now! You are going to walk this path as long as it takes for God's purposes to be accomplished in your life, so you might as well decide to hear what He has to say and do what He wants to do, right?

From the moment you accepted Jesus Christ as your Lord and Savior, the Bible says that God began a good work in you and that He will carry it out until completion until the day of Christ Jesus. God always finishes what He starts! I also want to encourage you to believe that God knows what He's doing, and that no matter what your circumstances are or how you feel, He is going to lead you step by step. But you have got to trust Him.

A man's steps are directed by the Lord. How then can anyone understand his own way? (Proverbs 20:24).

God's Plan of Salvation

If by chance you do not know the joy of the Lord firsthand, it is no accident or coincidence that you picked up this book to read during a crisis period in your life, one that leaves you rattled to the core and very afraid of what the future may hold. Maybe someone you know gave you this book to read, in hopes that it will provide useful tips for surviving a layoff until your next job appears.

Do you feel as though you are sinking in quicksand? God's love is the only rope you will ever need—the only rope that can truly save you, not only from yourself, but also from the things of this world.

Please consider where you are in life today and all of the events that led up to now. Maybe you know the Lord, and maybe you don't.

With all of the uncertainty life offers, from living in a post-September 11 world, the Columbia space-shuttle tragedy, the war in Iraq, and now continued threats of terrorism, if you were to pass away tonight in your sleep, do you know where you would spend eternity? Wouldn't you like to know for sure?

The truth is, God is our Divine Employer. He has an exciting job for you to do while on Earth, that only you can do. In addition, you can't beat out on His retirement package! Let's look at a few pertinent truths found in God's Word:

> *For God so loved the world that He gave His one and only Son, that whoever believes in Him shall not perish but have eternal life. (John 3:16)*

> *But now a righteousness from God, apart from law, has been made known, to which the Law and the Prophets testify. This righteousness from God comes through faith in Jesus Christ to all who believe. There is no difference, for all have sinned and fall short of the glory of God, and are justified freely by his grace through the redemption that came by Christ Jesus. God presented him as a sacrifice of atonement, through faith in his blood.... (Romans 3:21-25)*

> *But God demonstrates his own love for us in this: While we were still sinners, Christ died for us. (Romans 5:8)*

> *Yet to all who received him, to those who believed in his name, he gave the right to become children of God—children born not of natural descent, nor of human decision or a husband's will, but born of God. (John 1:12-13)*

All God asks of you is this: to acknowledge Jesus Christ as your Lord and Savior, repent of your sins, and invite Him into your heart. If you want the rest—the peace, the joy, and the strength that only a personal relationship with Jesus Christ can bring—why not pray a simple prayer, something like this:

"God, I have heard about you all my life and have run from you every time. I recognize the sacrifice you have made for me by sending your only Son, Jesus Christ, to die on the Cross for my sins—past, present, and future.

Lord, I have nowhere else to go but into your arms as the sinner that I am. Please forgive me for everything I have ever said or done that was not pleasing in your eyes, and help me to start fresh from this moment forward. Please come into my life and direct my paths, as you have promised to do. Open the eyes of my heart and help me to understand the truths of your Word. Thank you for coming to save me. I ask for this prayer to be answered through Jesus Christ. Amen."

If you have prayed this prayer, let me be the first to congratulate you! Please share this good news with another person, preferably a Christian friend or family member. If there is no one like that in your life right now, run—don't walk—to your nearest church and talk to the pastor. I know from experience that the Lord will place exactly the right people into your life to minister to you during this time and help you develop a personal relationship with Jesus Christ.

Scripture to Help You Turn To and Trust God

Do not let your hearts be troubled. Trust in God; trust also in me. (John 14:1)

The Lord is near to all who call on Him, to all who call on Him in truth. He fulfills the desires of those who fear Him; He hears their cry and saves them. The Lord watches over all who love Him, but all the wicked He will destroy. (Psalm 145:18-20)

The Lord will guide you always; He will satisfy your needs in a sun-scorched land and will strengthen your frame. You will be like a well-watered garden, like a spring whose waters never fail. (Isaiah 58:11)

For he will deliver the needy who cry out, the afflicted who have no one to help. (Psalm 72:12)

The Lord is righteous in all his ways and loving toward all He has made. The Lord is near to all who call on Him, to all who call on Him in truth. (Psalm 145:17-18)

CHAPTER TWO

Creating Sanity in a New Reality

Trust in the Lord with all your heart and lean not on your own understanding. In all your ways acknowledge Him, and He will make your paths straight.
Proverbs 3:5-6

You—like me—have two choices on how best to respond to your layoff. First, we can wallow in grief, anger and hopelessness forever, wasting valuable time and energy in the process. Or we can commit in our hearts, souls, minds and spirits to trust God to provide for and protect us, now and forevermore. Take comfort in the fact that even while we sleep, God watches over us. He never rests. He always has His eye on us, and God always wants what is best for us. But we need to cooperate with Him to receive it.

He will not let your foot slip—He who watches over you will not slumber; indeed, He who watches over Israel will neither slumber nor sleep. (Psalm 121:3-4)

Tools of the Trade

No matter what you have done in the past to earn your own way, your layoff has caused you to need a new set of tools for the trade—regardless of what it is. The tools you will need include faith, wisdom, and discernment.

What is faith? Hebrews 11:1 says, "Now faith is being sure of what we hope for and certain of what we do not see." What that means is that regardless of how we feel, we believe and act upon what God's Word says. Without faith in God, we might as well punch out on the time clock for good.

One way to get faith is to ask for it. Jesus tells us in John 15:7, "If you remain in me and my words remain in you, ask whatever you wish, and it will be given you." Be warned, however, that God is not some celestial Santa Claus. He will not give you anything He knows will harm you. Our Father wants us to rely on Him to meet all of our needs, and the only way to do that is for us to fall back into His arms. God loves you, my friend, and if you will ask for what you do not have, He will give it to you as long as He knows it is in your best interest and is in line with His will for your life. Besides, Matthew 6:8 tells us that God knows what we need before we ask Him. So, we might as well ask and receive.

> *And without faith it is impossible to please God, because anyone who comes to Him must believe that He exists and that He rewards those who earnestly seek Him. (Hebrews 11:6)*

Okay, what if you've been a believer for years, and are struggling with shame for doubting your faith, which perhaps you've never really needed until now? You won't be the first person to feel this way.

The Apostle Mark writes in chapter nine about a demon-possessed boy and his father who is desperate to find help for him. In the middle of a crowd, the father speaks to Jesus and after describing his son's condition, says:

> *But if you can do anything, take pity on us and help us! And Jesus said to him, If you can? All things are possible to him who believes. Immediately the boy's father cried and said, I do believe; help me overcome my unbelief! (Mark 9:21-24).*

Friends, I have asked God to help my unbelief many times, and He has helped me every time. Not some of the time—every time. You have nothing to be ashamed of if your faith is shaky, so don't go on some unnecessary guilt trip. Confess it to God and ask Him to help increase your faith. He is faithful and will be happy to answer that prayer.

Wisdom and discernment are interchangeable tools designed for use in making decisions about which jobs to apply for, whether to relocate, how to determine the right job offer, and so on. As with all things we need, we must ask God for wisdom and discernment.

God is omnipotent, omnipresent, and omniscient. He is the Creator of all things, He knows all things, and He is in control of all things. There is no one—and nothing—greater or wiser, more loving or more powerful than He. No, not even you. So why *wouldn't* you want to speed past "Go" and turn directly to Him for answers and for help?

> *If any of you lacks wisdom, he should ask God, who gives generously to all without finding fault, and it will be given to him. But when he asks, he must believe and not doubt, because he who doubts is like a wave of the sea, blown and tossed by the wind. (James 1:5-6)*

> *I guide you in the way of wisdom and lead you along straight paths. When you walk, your steps will not be hampered; when you run, you will not stumble. Hold on to instruction, do not let it go; guard it well, for it is your life. (Proverbs 4:11-13)*

Seeking God's Will

Understand that in order for God to help you, you must first surrender your life and everything in it. As silly as it sounds, you must—for all intended purposes—give God permission to be your Supervisor. God loves all of us so much that He gave us free will to make decisions on our own, including how we want to live our lives. The Lord is a gentleman, He will never force himself on you or anyone else. How would you like it if you had to force your own children to love you? Since we are His children, why would God feel any different about us?

One of the best ways to get God's help is to get down on your knees and ask for it. In 1 Peter 5:6-7 the Bible says:

> *Humble yourselves; therefore, under God's mighty hand, that He may lift you up in due time.*

Cast all your anxiety on Him because He cares for you.

The book of Psalms is filled with prayers you can pray straight from the Bible if you are unsure how to pray. "Answer me when I call to you, O my righteous God. Give me relief from my distress; be merciful to me and hear my prayer," writes David, in Psalm 4:1. "Know that the Lord has set apart the godly for himself; the Lord will hear when I call to Him" (Psalm 4:3).

Whether you are a new Christian or a veteran believer, spending time in the book of Psalms is, in my experience, what brings me the most comfort, hope and healing, especially during a layoff. The prayers are so relevant to what so many of us are feeling, and every time I read and pray them aloud to God, my faith is renewed, my hope is restored, and I am able to continue pressing on with joy in spite of my circumstances.

God is up to something good in your life. Perhaps He is working in your life as a vinedresser, or gardener, wanting to help you rid yourself of things, people, or wrong attitudes in your life that are harmful to you and have, so far, thwarted His purposes for your life. "I am the true vine, and my Father is the gardener. He cuts off every branch in me that bears no fruit, while every branch that does bear fruit He prunes so that it will be even more fruitful," states John 15:1-2.

Isaiah 64:8 reminds us:

Yet, O Lord, you are our Father. We are the clay, you are the potter; we are all the work of your hand." God is using this life experience to *mold and shape you into the beautiful creation He knows you can be.*

God, as our Good Shepherd, is also teaching us to hear and respond to His voice. "I am the good shepherd; I know my sheep and my sheep know me—just as the Father knows me and I know the Father—and I lay down my life for the sheep. I have other sheep that are not of this sheep pen; I must bring them also. They too will listen to my voice, and there shall be one flock and one shepherd" (John 10:14-16).

In addition to teaching us to hear and follow His voice, God as our Shepherd seeks to protect us from harm, and especially, Satan. "Be self-controlled and alert. Your enemy the devil prowls around like a roaring lion looking for someone to devour" (1 Peter 5:8). Boy, that's an understatement.

Obedience: A Command, Not an Option

There is no point in seeking God's will if you are not willing to be obedient to whatever He calls you to do, especially when it doesn't make sense in the secular world. Do everything that God asks you to do—not just the easy things! Obeying God, especially when we don't feel like it, is what produces Godly character. Efforts to be obedient in our own strength will fail, but like the Apostle Paul writes, "I can do all things through Christ who strengthens me" (Philippians 4:13, NKJV).

God's blessings come only to those who not only *read* His Word, but also *do* what it says. Think about it. If you are a parent, are you going to give your son a new bicycle when he refuses to keep his room clean like you've asked? No. God—as our heavenly Father—is no different.

When we are not being obedient to God, we are not only hurting Him, we are hurting ourselves. Why would any of us, including myself, want to be disobedient? Because obedience isn't always fun, that's why. We might as well do what He wants us to do; otherwise, He'll send us back into the classroom again and again until we get it. To put it another way, if we know we're going to experience pain whether we remain the same and nothing changes, or we know we're going to benefit from the pain because God is working in us, and either way we're going to hurt, why not experience *productive* pain? It is going to hurt no matter what, so why not get something good out of it at the end, as God promises?

Because of the stubbornness in their hearts, the Israelites roamed in the desert for forty years before behaving, though Jonah spent only three days in the belly of a fish before he admitted his mistakes. Just as the sooner our children finish their homework, they can go outside and play, the sooner we do what God is asking of us, the sooner we are delivered from our circumstances.

Repent, Repent, Repent

No one likes to think they may have sins they haven't confessed, but often times we do and may not realize it. Maybe God is trying to get your attention on a particular sin in your life and has allowed or even caused this layoff as a way for you to open your spiritual eyes and look into your heart, as He does.

What are you going to do—run *from* Him, or run *to* Him? Lest you think you can handle this adversity on your own, Solomon wisely warns us, "Pride goes before destruction, a haughty spirit before a fall" (Proverbs 16:18). Do not place your trust in yourself or someone else, because we're all faulty human beings. Let the words of a popular Christian song ring true in your heart and soul: "God is God, and I am not."

Let's look at the value of repentance, based on the life of David, who was a man after God's own heart.

David's Nosedive Into Sin

After committing adultery with Bathsheba, David soon learned that she had conceived and eventually bore his child. Rather than immediately take responsibility, recognize and repent of his sin, he arranged to have Bathsheba's husband, Uriah, murdered and then tried to hide his crime.

The Lord waited for David to recognize his sins on his own and repent, but that didn't happen. The prophet Nathan was sent to David with a parable of sorts, to which David "burned with anger" against the man Nathan spoke of in the parable (2 Samuel 12:5). Nathan told David, "You are the man!" (2 Samuel 12:7). He went on to warn David that God was going to punish him for his sin, if he didn't 'fess up.

> *This is what the Lord says: Out of your household I am going to bring calamity upon you. Before your very eyes I will take your wives and give them to one who is close to you, and he will lie with your wives in broad daylight. You did it in secret, but I will do this thing in broad daylight before all Israel. (2 Samuel 12:11-12)*

When David heard this, he was grieved of his sin and immediately confessed it to the Lord, who in turn, forgave him immediately—but not without consequences. David bore the price for his sins by losing his baby shortly thereafter. God eventually blessed David and Bathsheba again through the birth of a new son, Solomon, who many consider to be one of the wisest men in the Bible.

Dangers of Unconfessed Sin
Maybe you have sinned—intentionally or unintentionally—and God has allowed this experience to occur in order for you to take some serious stock in yourself, your life, family, and most importantly, your relationship with Him.

Sin is bad for us. It breaks fellowship with God, and without that fellowship, how else will we hear His voice when He speaks? I can think of nothing more frightening than being separated from God. The Lord absolutely wants what is best for us, but we must humble ourselves, ask Him to point out our sins so that we can repent and receive forgiveness, and get on the right path with God.

> *If we claim to be without sin, we deceive ourselves and the truth is not in us. If we confess our sins, He is faithful and just and will forgive us our sins and purify us from all unrighteousness. If we claim we have not sinned, we make Him out to be a liar and His Word has no place in our lives. (1 John 1:8-10)*

> *Search me, O God, and know my heart; test me and know my anxious thoughts. See if there is*

any offensive way in me, and lead me in the way everlasting. (Psalm 139:23-24)

All of us are sinners, we all fall short of the glory of God. Even upon confessing and repenting of our sins, there are consequences to our actions.

Perhaps you were really, really good at your former job, and it inflated your ego a bit too much. Pride is a sin. Maybe you allowed work to take over your life and it took you away from your spouse and kids. Was that job an idol in your life, did it give you a false illusion that you were in control of all things, instead of God? Idolatry is a sin.

Rest assured that whatever the reason—whether it is one day revealed to you or not—know that God wants to use this layoff for your good and His glory if you'll let Him. But you must turn to and trust God because He knows what He's doing, even if you don't.

The good news is that all of our sins—past, present, and future—were paid for at the cross by Jesus Christ. I can never stop thanking Him for this.

Praise God for Who He Is—Not What He Can Do

Despite how this layoff is causing you to feel toward God, you need to praise Him now more than ever. If you don't feel like praising Him, ask Him to help you do so. Although I learned through my first layoff (1994-1996) and continue to learn how much God loves me, and although my faith is stronger today than it has ever been, there are times when I am so tired of being without a job that I become overwrought with despair.

There are days I lay face down in my living room, crying so hard that I feel surely the foundation will begin to sink, my heart is so heavy in pain. It doesn't mean I don't trust God. I do. But sometimes it hurts. I have been so broken that in my pain I cannot even pray, other than to whimper, "God."

I beg Him for the peace that surpasses all understanding, and like being covered with a blanket by a loved one, He gives it to me. I remind myself of His faithfulness during the first layoff and in my life ever since, and I'm able to stand. I know that no weapon formed against me shall prosper, that greater is He who is in me than he who is of this world, that God has never and will never leave me nor forsake me. I look at page after page in my prayer journal, seeing written evidence of my own prayers answered, and my spirit soars until I can do nothing but lift my voice to Him in praise, thanking Him for allowing me to experience His indescribable presence once again.

I may not have a job, and I certainly don't have financial security now or in my foreseeable future. Yet, I—like you, if you have trusted Jesus Christ as your Savior—have all I need. Regardless of how stark the landscape of your life is, you hold on. Do not give up on God. I have learned in my walk with the Lord that often times, the greater the pain, the greater the gain in the long run. I once heard a pastor say that when one of Jesus' sheep cries, He stops first, listens to discern who is crying, and then *runs* to help us. What a great visual.

Now, why praise God when He's allowing us to hurt so much? Because He is worthy to be praised, that's why. There is no one on Earth who will love you more and take care of you better than He. If it weren't for God, you wouldn't have your family and friends, your home, your car, your health, the clothes on your back, the food on your table, and, yes, even the skills God gave you to earn a living to begin with.

> *Praise the Lord, O my soul; all my inmost being, praise His holy name. Praise the Lord, O my soul, and forget not all His benefits—who forgives all your sins and heals all your diseases, who redeems your life from the pit and crowns you with love and compassion, who satisfies your desires with good things so that your youth is renewed like the eagle's. (Psalm 103:1-5)*

Have a Grateful Heart

While it may be hard to do, learn to recognize and count out loud the blessings you have right now. If you and your family have food to eat, clothes to wear, and a roof over your heads—even if you don't have the money to pay for those things today—thank God for them. God promises to provide for our every need, right? We need food, clothing, and shelter. But most of all, we need Him.

Let's not be like the ungrateful Israelites in the Old Testament, pouting like no tomorrow because life wasn't a day at the beach all the time. Poor Moses was led with the task of leading them out of the desert and onward to the land of milk and honey. After the miraculous parting of the Red Sea, God allowed the Israelites to cross over to safety in the nick of time. Afterward, God used His power to let the sea's walls fall again, allowing all of Pharaoh and his army, who were in hot pursuit of the Israelites, to drown. Those ungrateful Israelites *still* griped! If we are to be honest, there are times when we are no better than they.

Interesting enough, shortly after this experience, they entered into the Desert of Sin, where Moses writes that the whole community was grumbling against him and Aaron, whining, "If only we had died by the Lord's hand in Egypt! There we sat around pots of meat and ate all the food we wanted, but you have brought us out into the desert to starve this entire assembly to death" (Exodus 16:3).

Watch how God responded:

> *Then the Lord said to Moses, I will rain down bread from Heaven for you. The people are to go out each day and gather enough for that day. In this way I will test them and see whether they follow my instructions. On the sixth day they are to prepare what they bring in, and that is to be twice as much as they gather on other days. (Exodus 16:4-5)*

Be grateful for what you have. It is my prayer that—like the Apostle Paul—you will learn to be content in whatever circumstances you are faced with. Talk about a guy who had it bad! Paul had been beaten, chased, and thrown in prison, among other things, all because of his love for the Lord. Yet still, he approached his circumstances like, "No problem, man. With God, I'm cool."

> *I have learned the secret of being content in any and every situation, whether fed or hungry, whether living in plenty or in want. I can do everything through Him who gives me strength. (Philippians 4:12-13)*

Have you been chased down the street lately for the sake of the Lord? Have you been starved, beaten, and thrown in prison for the sake of the Lord, or for any other reason, for that matter? Probably not. We may *think* we have it bad, trying to make ends meet without a job, but our suffering pales in comparison to Paul's. Far more importantly, it will never compare to the suffering Jesus Christ endured at the hands of those who beat Him and nailed Him to a Cross where He died for us. Complaining doesn't produce anything but a sour attitude, hardened heart and self-pity, none of which are qualities a prospective employer wants to see!

We are to give thanks to God in *all* circumstances. Consider Job, a righteous, blameless man in the eyes of the Lord, who—for no apparent reason he could see—lost everything he owned: his children, his livestock, his servants, his home, his health. Yet, Job's response was amazing:

> *Shall we accept good from God, and not trouble? (Job 2:10)*

Job suffered for what must have seemed like an eternity, with even his close friends and his own wife mocking him, accusing him of unconfessed sin and all but blaming him for his troubles. Yet, not once did Job sin in his responses to them. In the end, God rewarded Job for his faithfulness by multiplying everything he had lost.

> *Sing and make music in your heart to the Lord, always giving thanks to God the Father for everything, in the name of our Lord Jesus Christ. (Ephesians 5:19-20)*

> *Every good and perfect gift is from above, coming down from the Father of the heavenly lights, who does not change like shifting shadows. (James 1:17)*

Am I discounting that you have a right to not feel terribly excited about your circumstances? No. Remember, I'm in the trenches with you, and I have a bum knee in constant pain. If you're having trouble finding gratitude right now, don't feel bad. God understands. Prayer works wonders, mi amigo. Why not stop right now and confess your ungrateful heart to God, and ask Him to change it to reflect His goodness. God always answers prayers, especially urgent ones.

My prayer for you is that you learn to give thanks to God for all that you have, the person you are, and the person He is molding, shaping, and refining you to be. God is here with you now, as He is here with me now, and He *is* taking care of us. God is our Father, and we are His children, enough said.

The Power of Speaking God's Word Out Loud

The tongue is an awfully small body part, but boy is it powerful when used in the right way. The Bible says that with it, the tongue has the power of life and death, and that those who love it will eat its fruit. We are instructed to call things forth that are not, as though they were. This means that often times, whatever we say out loud will manifest itself in the future.

The more we read God's Word and speak it out in our daily lives, the more God will be able to use His power in our lives. Write out certain Scriptures that are meaningful to you and memorize them. If you seek God and His righteousness first, all you need will be given to you. I speak from experience—heart knowledge and not head knowledge. This is not my first time at the fair, my friend.

There is a multitude of amazing Scriptures concerning wisdom, discernment, knowledge, understanding, self-control, patience, and so much more that you can speak out loud each day as part of your prayer time. It is a great way to memorize Scripture, too!

CHAPTER THREE

Your Job Is to Find a Job

*The laborer's appetite works for him;
his hunger drives him on.*
Proverbs 16:26

Looking for a job is often times more difficult than having one, I think because of the uncertainty that comes with unemployment. At least when you *have* a job, you know what to expect. You know where you are going each day, what you will do when you get there, and that in a matter of another week or so, you will get a paycheck.

The task of looking for work in today's job market, especially if you're still in shock or dealing with feelings of anger and grief, can be quite daunting. This chapter will take you step-by-step through the steps God has given me to follow immediately after my layoff.

Filing for Unemployment
Nine chances out of ten, if you have been laid off as a reduction of workforce, you are eligible to receive

unemployment compensation. Call your local unemployment office or visit its website to get started. The sooner you get your information into the system, the sooner you will probably receive benefits.

Organization: It Can Happen to You

Okay, now is the time to get organized. One of the first things you must do is set up your own version of Command Central. Despite your impending financial diet, if you don't have a desk at home, go spend about thirty bucks on a long folding table to serve as a holding place for a fax machine, calendar, paper trays, and Rolodex. Everything you need for your job search will be on this table.

Next, buy a notebook or binder for use in keeping track of all advertisements for employment that you respond to. Once you cut the ads out, tape them onto the pages, and next to each ad, write the date you responded. That way when companies call for interviews or more information, it will be easy to identify which ad they are referring to when they call. As you get rejection slips from these ads, simply mark an "X" through the ad and thank God for not sending you to the wrong job! Or, if you're a computer geek, start an Excel or Word file listing the same information.

Buying a fax machine will pay for itself in no time. At first I hesitated on making this purchase, because I felt it was not a "need," but a "want." However, after spending less than $100 on a very basic model, I found it to be almost as useful as my computer. Not only is the cost of a fax machine a write-off under the "job search" category for income tax purposes, the money and time you save by not driving to a facility to pay for the use of their fax machine is worth it.

Closed Doors Mean Open Windows

Many times people have said that when God closes a door, He opens a window. Being laid off is not the end of the world and you *will* find employment again. Decide if what you were doing before is what you want to be doing the rest of your life. There is no law that says you have to do the same line of work for the rest of your life, just because it's what you've always done. Unless, of course, you love what you've been doing!

If you could be successful at doing one thing, what would it be? What floats your boat? What does your dream job look like? What are your hobbies and interests? Have you come up with any answers? If so, now is the time to create two or even three resumes, depending on what your hopes and dreams are with regard to your next position.

Highlight your experience and qualities up front on the first page. Ask yourself what types of skills and experience are necessary for any possible career change you may be seeking and see if you don't possess a few of them to put down. I suspect that if you're following your heart's desire this time, you will have more than a few bullet points to list. After all, God gives us talents and skills to use, and He places a dream in our hearts to do so.

"Job seekers need to talk up their transferable skills to match the job criteria," explained Colleen Madden, research consultant at Challenger, Gray & Christmas.

"Having a few variations of your resume to specific jobs is also advisable," she continued.

When you step out in faith and believe you are being led by the Holy Spirit to do something, and you make a mistake, God will save you at the last minute before disaster strikes. But don't stand still in a frozen state, afraid of your shadow.

As an example, one morning about three months after I was laid off for this second and current time, before my feet ever hit the ground, I heard a voice in my spirit that told me to put my house up for sale. It didn't make sense to do this, because I had no job and no job prospects at the time, although I had been applying for jobs all over the country.

I believed with all my heart that it was God telling me to do this because sometimes He asks us to step out in faith and do really crazy things that don't make sense. In my mind, I thought it was His way not only of testing my obedience, but also preparing the way for me to have the house sold right at the same time my big job offer would come in.

Although I was quick to jump the gun, I sought the advice of two pastors. One said to go for it, the other cautioned against it. Ultimately I chose to put it on the market, because our senior pastor has instructed us in the past that if we honestly and truly believe that we hear from God then we should do what He says, even if it goes against the godly counsel we receive.

My family and friends were more distraught than I was over the thought of my losing this house less than two years after I bought it. I, on the other hand, was skipping in glee because I just *knew* that I had heard from God and He was going to send me my job soon!

Two months passed before I had a serious interested potential buyer. Suddenly the reality of losing this house, having to relocate my daughter and me to different places to live, all without a job, hit me. I became very scared and very depressed and explained to one of my pastors what I had done.

"You did not hear from God," he said, explaining that God is a God of order, and that the job would come first and *then* I should put the house up for sale. On the one hand, I was elated because I never really wanted to sell the house to begin with. But remember, life is not about what we want; it's about what God wants *for* us. Secondly, I was so afraid that my abilities to hear from God were off.

"Satan comes as an angel of light to steal, kill and destroy," he continued. "God intervened at the last minute so you would not lose your house." It turns out that the buyer wasn't qualified, so she wouldn't have gotten the sale anyway. Praise God!

God will make something good out of your mistake, as long as He can see you are seeking Him in all you do. Paul writes in Romans 8:28, "And we know that in all things God works for the good of those who love Him, for those who have been called according to His purpose." You cannot lose if you step out in faith, either way.

Only you and God know what it is you really want to do for a living, so get off the fence and get to work. Write out on paper what steps you need to take to make that dream a reality. Then follow them, especially if you're afraid. Go for it.

Commit to the Lord whatever you do, and your plans will succeed. (Proverbs 16:3)

Temporary Employment and Internships

As soon as you have time, register with several temporary employment agencies. Make an appointment, go in and fill out the appropriate paperwork, and make yourself available as often as possible to work. The more money you are able to earn on your own, the longer your unemployment benefits will last and the better you will feel about yourself. I know many people who started out working for a company as a contract employee and ended up being offered a full-time job. It's a great way to maintain your skills, meet people, and earn money.

Most people associate the concept of internships with college-aged students, but not anymore.

"We're definitely seeing a trend of more seasoned workers moving into unpaid internships to shore up their knowledge base, usually to learn new technologies and business practices. Part-time paid positions or paid internships are another way older job seekers are learning new skills while still bringing in some income," Madden said.

There may be some challenges in seeking and accepting part-time employment. Employers may be hesitant to hire someone overqualified, and accepting part-time work may hurt a job seeker's sense of pride. "Age bias does permeate the workplace, especially in industries that normally see college-age workers.

"Competition for all kinds of jobs is fierce. Older job seekers are going to have to tap into their extensive professional wisdom to land a position, whether as a part-time employee, intern, or otherwise," she continued.

Using the Internet

The Internet is the easiest, quickest, most productive and time-saving way to look for work. Most libraries offer free access to computers if you do not own one. Ask for help if you need it. Search for employment agencies in your area, then log onto their websites to enter your resume and contact information. Many have free job email notification services that contact you each time a job matching your chosen criteria and qualifications becomes available.

The process is a bit time-consuming, but it's worth it in the long run. Each morning when you log on, there will be emails containing links to jobs that you may be qualified to do. All you have to do now is click the links, decide if you're qualified and interested, and forward you resume. It's that simple, and it sure beats having to subscribe to a number of newspapers across the country to get the same information!

When responding to an ad via email, it is best to copy and paste your resume within the email rather than sending as an attachment, because many companies are afraid of viruses being attached to files. If possible, create or have someone create a website for you where prospective employers can learn more about you.

Help for the Laid Off

Network, Network, Network

Establishing and nurturing business relationships is crucial to your career, both now and in the future. One of the best tips I ever learned when I began my career as a journalist was to, as soon as possible after meeting someone and receiving their business card, write the date on the back of the card, along with the location and circumstances of the meeting. When in the future I needed to contact them, I was able to say, "We met last April at the 'XYZ' conference in London," as a way of giving me credibility before making my request.

Now is the time to send your resume out to every person you've ever done business with, either personally or professionally. Write up a great cover letter (reintroducing yourself if necessary), explain what has happened and that you are including a copy of your resume for their consideration for future positions. If you don't have a cell phone, get one—that that way you have mobility in your life and are not chained to the house, afraid to leave for five minutes like I used to be years ago.

Look to your church family for help. Many churches offer job placement or career advice ministry services. If I were a Christian employer, where better to find a good employee than through my own church family?

Get yourself an inexpensive set of business cards printed. I paid $11 for a box of a thousand plain white business cards that have my name, phone numbers (home, cell, and fax) and email address. You never know who you're going to meet, and at this price, you can't afford to be without them. It's an easy, professional way to hand over your contact information.

Join a Support Group

Considering the amount of people being laid off worldwide, chances are there are job loss support groups available at many churches. Joining a job loss support group is something to consider, although they are not for everyone. By having a regular meeting date and others to talk to who are walking the same lonely path, this phase of your life may not be as difficult as it would be otherwise.

The Importance of Saving Receipts

Go to your nearest office supply store and spend $5 on a pocket-sized mileage log to keep in your vehicle. By writing down the mileage driven every time you go on a job interview, to the post office, office supply store, etc.—i.e. anything that has to do with looking for a job—you can deduct the year-end figure off of your taxes. Other receipts you should be saving include those for postage, office equipment, cellular phone service, Internet services, newspaper subscriptions, professional association dues, office supplies, long distance calls, and more. All of these can be deducted from your taxes at the end of the year. Finally, a benefit to being laid off!

Buy yourself a portable filing case and fill it with folders for each receipt category, in addition to one for your unemployment benefits check statements and medical bills incurred while you are laid off. You will need all of this information when filing your taxes, so it is convenient to have everything you need at your fingertips at a moment's notice.

Lazy hands make a man poor, but diligent hands bring wealth. (Proverbs 10:4)

Preparing for a Job Interview

Many employers seek the same information and ask many similar questions of their job applicants. Think ahead, and prepare answers to questions like:

1. Why did you leave your last company?
2. Where do you see yourself five or 10 years from now?
3. What are your career goals? What are you good at?
4. If you could do anything successfully, what would it be, and why?
5. Are you willing to relocate?
6. What skills, experience and abilities do you offer that perhaps our other candidates do not?
7. Why do you want to work for me and/or this company?
8. When can you begin work?
9. What is the biggest mistake you've ever made in your career, and how did you rectify it? What did you learn from it?
10. What is your working style, i.e. do you prefer to work independently, with a group, and/or be micromanaged?

Before you walk in the door of the interview room or before you pick up the receiver to answer that telephone interview phone call, be sure to pray to God for guidance, wisdom, discernment, and the ability to answer questions clearly, calmly, and concisely. Consider the question and think before you speak. Try not to talk too fast, and leave out the "ums," which most of us utter to fill dead air space. Finally, always tell the truth, not only because it is the right thing to do, but also because all things hidden are eventually uncovered.

Mind Your Manners!
Good manners never go out of style, and what better way to strengthen your witness to Christians and non-believers, than to get into the habit of sending thank-you notes in the mail. Through the U.S. postal system, that is.

Tasteful boxed sets of thank-you notes can be purchased at any large chain store for under $5, and they are worth the expense (in addition to being another tax write-off). After each interview, whether in person or by telephone, always send a hand-written thank-you note to the person you interviewed with. Some things never go out of style, and everyone likes to receive something nice in the mail besides bills! Now those who know me know I'm hardly Ms. Etiquette, but for what it's worth, I don't think it's a good idea to email a thank-you note: It's too easy and not personal enough.

CHAPTER FOUR

Spending Your Spare Time

*Be anxious for nothing, but in everything
by prayer and supplication with thanksgiving
let your requests be made known to God.*
Philippians 4:6

With the tools of the trade underneath your belt or in your purse, you are ready to begin creating a new daily routine in addition to searching for work. By creating some kind of order to your life, it will help you feel more in control and more productive in efforts to become gainfully employed. Below are my suggestions on how to spend your spare time.

The Importance of Prayer
Nothing you can do in your walk with the Lord is more important than praying on a daily basis, and it should be the first thing you do each morning. Prayer is our way of directly communicating with God, and it is the only way to build and maintain a close relationship with Him. You cannot—and will not—be able to have a peaceful and

productive day without conversing with God and asking Him exactly how He wants you to spend each day, whom you should contact, and what lessons you can learn from the day's events and other people.

While He was on Earth, Jesus prayed on a regular basis for the peace, comfort, strength, and guidance He needed from our God and Father. There are several examples of this found in the New Testament.

After feeding five thousand men, in addition to women and children, Jesus commanded His disciples to get into a boat and go out into the water before Him. Matthew 14:23 states, "After he had dismissed them, He went up on a mountainside by himself to pray. When evening came, He was there alone."

Later on, shortly before the events leading up to His arrest and crucifixion, Matthew 26:36 says: "Then Jesus went with his disciples to a place called Gethsemane, and he said to them, 'Sit here while I go over there and pray.'" Peter and the two sons of Zebedee went with Jesus, who became very distraught. Jesus let them know that He was "overwhelmed with sorrow to the point of death," and asked them to stay and keep watch with Him (Matthew 26:37-38).

"Going a little farther, he fell with his face to the ground and prayed, 'My Father, if it is possible, may this cup be taken from me. Yet not as I will, but as you will'" (Matthew 26:39). Jesus knew what was getting ready to go down. Can you just imagine how scared He was? How arrogant of anyone to think they do not need to pray. If Jesus needed to pray, then so do I, and so do you!

It is important to note that Jesus prayed for God's will to be done and not His own. Therefore, we should follow His example. God is going before you every step of this layoff, and it is important to pray as Jesus did: for God to ignore your will and allow His.

The Book of Psalms is packed with beautiful prayers, many of them written by David and his son, Solomon. I like to begin each day by praying the words found in Psalm 51:10-12, which says:

> *Create in me a pure heart, O God, and renew a steadfast spirit within me. Do not cast me away from your presence, and do not take your Holy Spirit from me. Restore me to the joy of your salvation, and grant me a willing spirit, to sustain me.*

More than anything else though, God wants us to speak to Him from our hearts and tell Him everything. The Lord already knows what our needs are before we ask Him, yet He wants us to learn to be totally dependent upon Him for all things through prayer.

> *Be joyful in hope, patient in affliction, faithful in prayer. (Romans 12:12)*

ACTS is a great acronym for prayer. It goes like this:

A—*Acknowledge* God for all that He is: holy, omnipotent, omnipresent, and omniscient, the Creator of all things and the most powerful and wise being there ever was and will be.

C—*Confess* your sins, repent of them, and ask for and receive forgiveness.

T—*Thank* God for all that He has blessed you with and even for allowing this adversity into your life.

Whether you realize it right now or not, He is working great things in your life!

S—*Supplication:* Ask God to supply what you need to make it through the day.

Did you know that prayer (and praise and worship) is a mighty weapon in spiritual warfare? Prayer often changes God's mind about your circumstances or the circumstances of those you are praying for. Our God is a good and mighty God, He is our Father, and He wants so much to bless us. But He wants us to ask for what we want, first.

Even at times when you are so discouraged that you don't know what to pray for, don't worry. After Jesus died and rose again, He sent us the Holy Spirit to live inside every believer. Check this out:

> *We do not know what we ought to pray for, but the Spirit himself intercedes for us with groans that words cannot express. And he who searches our hearts knows the mind of the Spirit, because the Spirit intercedes for the saints in accordance with God's will. (Romans 8:26-27)*

If Jesus thought it was important enough to pray while He was with us on Earth, and if the Holy Spirit intercedes on our behalf when we are in such pain that we are speechless, I would submit to start praying every day!

Exercise Your Body, Not Just Your Mind

Do you not know that your body is a temple of the Holy Spirit, who is in you, whom you have received from God? You are not your own; you were bought at a price. Therefore honor God with your body. (1 Corinthians 6:19-20)

Unless you've been sleeping all your waking life, I suspect you already know of the many benefits to be gained from participating in some form of physical exercise on a regular basis. Now more than ever, exercising is critical to your overall health and frame of mind.

Working out is not only good for you physically but also spiritually and mentally. It is a great time to pray and contemplate God's will in your life. Almost any excuse to get out of the house is a good one. Isolating yourself is an open invitation for Satan to walk through your door and life, and it magnifies any loneliness you may be feeling. How you exercise yourself (i.e. your "whole" self) is not the issue—what's important is that you get out there and move!

If you have any addictive behaviors, deal with them in a healthy manner rather than using them as a crutch to get you through this phase of your life. There are many support groups available, so ask someone at your church office to see if they offer any ministry services that meet your particular needs. Talk to friends, family, pastors, or family doctors and get the help you deserve. The Lord commands us to seek wise counsel, so do it!

To live a righteous and holy life before God, one of the things we must do as believers is to develop self-control, which is one of the fruits of the Holy Spirit listed in Galatians 5:22. If you do not have this particular fruit in your basket, ask the Holy Spirit to help you get it. He will. How do I know this, other than from personal experience? Because 1 John 5:14-15 states, "This is the confidence we have in approaching God: that if we ask anything according to his will, he hears us. And if we know that he hears us—whatever we ask—we know that we have what we asked of him." Need I say more?

Volunteering: Good for Everyone

Do nothing out of selfish ambition or vain conceit, but in humility consider others better than yourselves. Each of you should look not only to your own interests, but also to the interests of others. (Philippians 2:3-4)

One of the best ways to counteract depression and selfishness is by thinking of others and what we can do for them. If you look around your neighborhood and community, there is always someone who has it worse than you. In a perverse sort of way, some might consider this to be a good thing. I do not.

Once you have updated your resume and send it out to the masses each day, I can think of no better way to spend one's time while waiting for a job to show up than to start volunteering. Go to your church and volunteer at the reception desk, go visit someone in the hospital from your church family, sort clothes at a local Goodwill, deliver food to homebound senior citizens—do something.

Volunteering gives you a chance to get out of the house, help someone else less fortunate than you, and prevents you from wallowing in self-pity, while making you grateful for what you do have and helping you be productive by making the best use of your time. Even the Apostle Paul recommends it in the New Testament. Check it out:

> *Let us not become weary in doing good, for at the proper time we will reap a harvest if we do not give up. Therefore, as we have opportunity, let us do good to all people, especially to those who belong to the family of believers. (Galatians 6:9-10)*

Is Paul telling us to minister to only those who are already in Christ Jesus? No. God himself tells us that the greatest commandment of all is to love one another unconditionally. Correct me if I'm wrong, but this includes everyone—believers and non-believers alike. How else can we be salt and light to the world? How else will those who do not know Christ learn about Him through those of us who do?

If you continue to sit around the house after checking your email and reading the paper online looking for work, chances are you're going to turn into a zombie, gain a lot of weight, and allow lamebrain Satan a chance to get a stronghold in your life by pulling you down into the pit of despair. Satan hates you, my friend, and he is more than delighted to make you feel like a loser rather than the victor you are in Christ Jesus.

If you are a believer, you already have the power of Almighty God living inside you. Act like it.

Help for the Laid Off

Christian Counseling: A Very Good Thing

Several months after my first layoff in 1994, I felt as though I was in a locked room with no windows and the ceiling was closing in on me. I was afraid to leave the house, because with my luck that would be the time I missed a phone call about a job. Unemployment created a sense of captivity because I had no freedom. My mind and my emotions were muddled up, and they needed help. Thankfully there is Christian counseling available for times like that.

"When people come to a Christian counselor, they are often mad at God and want a safe place to be angry," said Moore. "They don't trust a secular counselor to keep them contained, and they do not want to be encouraged to reject God, but they do want the ability to vent in a safe Christian environment. Consequently, Scripture and prayer do not always fit into the equation until farther down the line. It would feel like preaching, and that isn't what they need or want at that time."

Perhaps this is your first experience with being laid off. Especially if you are a man, I cannot emphasize strongly enough how much I believe you would benefit from receiving counseling from another Christian, regardless of how strong you may or may not be in your walk with the Lord.

Today as I write these words, I'm looking out my window at the world, thinking of you. I hope and pray you will take what I am saying to heart. I would give anything to be sitting across from you, because if I were, I would take your hands in mine, look you directly in the face, and earnestly encourage you with all that I am and all that I have inside, to follow this advice. Pick up the phone and get on with it.

Do not be afraid or too proud to receive counseling.

Antidepressants: If You Need Them, Take Them

If you find yourself unable to get a good night's sleep, or you're crying at the drop of a hat and can't stop – please see your family doctor to ask if getting a prescription for antidepressants would be a good idea. There are plenty of safe medications they can give you to help stabilize your moods and sleep at night. Let's face it—we're not computers, we're humans.

It used to be in the good ole' days that we'd get up, shower, have breakfast, and go to work, at least secure in knowing we could provide for ourselves and our families. Now, as layoff victims, we're still responsible for caring for ourselves and our families, only now we can't do it because we have no place to go and no work to do.

It is a situation that would wear anyone down.

Reach Out to Your Family

While Christian counseling is something I wholeheartedly recommend, sometimes all you need is a loving family member on the other end of the phone. It's like my dad used to say: "Your blood runs through my veins." He would look straight into the eyes of all five of his kids and say this. I never understood the value of this until I really needed my family's help—when I could no longer take care of myself and Emilie.

Unfortunately, most times I know I don't reach out to them for emotional support often enough. Not because of pride, but because I love them too much to burden them with this unbearable weight. When you love someone, you don't want to hurt them by sharing with them just how hard it is to breathe sometimes. I know this will hurt them, and I don't want to do that.

However, I am beginning to learn that this is wrong because I'm cheating them out of the ability to help me by listening to me. When I am in pain, I don't want someone to cheer me up—I want them to L-I-S-T-E-N. I want them to *hear* me.

For example, a few months ago, I experienced the stupidest thing. I woke up, walked out onto the driveway to get my morning newspaper, and it was still dark out. I remembered how at that time of morning, I used to be out in my jogging suit walking the neighborhood before work.

After recalling what my normal schedule was like "in the good ole' days," my thoughts then turned to what my day was like when I got to the office. There was always a lot of laughter and it was a lot of fun to work with such wonderful, talented people. I "got to" go to work—that's how much fun it was! At least, until that fateful conference call when what I thought was going to end up as a promotion turned out to be a layoff.

Bad news is bad news, but for someone like me who loves people, enjoys her career, and thrives on being a productive member of society, for some reason, that morning, seeing all of my neighbors go off to their jobs like "normal people" just really got to me. I called my sister, Anne. It was the first time since I'd been laid off again that I really felt the sadness and pressure I was facing. Again.

Do you know that she stopped what she was doing and listened to me wail on the other end of the line, for at least thirty minutes? This may not sound like a big deal, but believe me, it meant everything to me. Anne's actions told me, "I love you, you are important to me, and I care that you are hurting. How can I help you?" I believe if I had needed her to listen to me for another hour, she would have canceled her meeting if that is what it took to lift me up.

I am going to trust that you will, at the very least, consider all that has been said here, and like me, do what you have to do. Talk to someone, and get antidepressants if necessary. If not for you, do it for your family. Don't worry, you will not be seen as weak, you will be seen as an intelligent, responsible person who recognizes the need for help, and gets it.

Chapter Five

Money Mattters

Command those who are rich in this present world not to be arrogant nor to put their hope in wealth, which is so uncertain, but to put their hope in God, who richly provides us with everything for our enjoyment.
1 Timothy 6:17

Now more than ever, it is critical that you make the most out of the money you currently have and will receive through unemployment and other various means. As hard as it is not to do, try not to feel sorry for yourself and go out and drop a ton of money on a luxury toy you cannot afford! In this chapter, I hope to offer sound advice regarding money: how to make it, keep it for as long as possible, and get the most out of your much-needed dollars.

The Importance of Tithing, Especially in Uncertain Times

For many of you, giving away money to the church during a time like this is terribly frightening. My friend, you are hurting yourself as well as sinning against God if you don't step out in faith—scary as it is—and hand over a minimum of 10 percent of your income.

Paul instructed the Corinthians with sound advice on the importance of tithing. In 2 Corinthians 9:6-8, he writes:

> *Remember this: Whoever sows sparingly will also reap sparingly, and whoever sows generously will also reap generously. Each man should give what he has decided in his heart to give, not reluctantly or under compulsion, for God loves a cheerful giver. And God is able to make all grace abound to you, so that in all things at all times, having all that you need, you will abound in every good work.*

There was a time when I would have been tempted not to tithe on my income, primarily out of fear. But not anymore.

Let me give you an example of how God honors His promises.

A few months ago, after having written checks for tithing and bills due, my checking account had a balance of $1.53. I was fine with this because for the moment, I had everything I needed for that day. I had not one thing to complain about, nor had I any reason to feel sorry for myself. In fact, I had much to be grateful for and was.

Lo and behold, I had some unexpected and large expenses arise. Rather than worry about how I was going to pay for them, rather than ask my family for even more money, I prayed and trusted God.

The floodgates from heaven opened within twenty-four hours in the form of a check from the benevolence fund from my church. A few days later I received checks from my family. Three of my dearest friends—Cathy, Deb, and Stella—gave me cash and paid my utilities.

Several weeks later, I was faced with the same situation with only $3.23 to my name after tithing on my unemployment check. Again I prayed, only this time I asked God for $500 because I knew my car note and other bills were nearly due. Within twenty-four hours, a pastor whom I did not know from my church called and asked me to meet him at church at two o'clock that afternoon, because he had a $600 check to give me. Not only did God answer my prayers for $500, but He also blessed me with an additional $100. Apparently someone shared my circumstances and needs with him at *precisely* the right time. Coincidence? No. God.

> *Give, and it will be given to you. A good measure, pressed down, shaken together and running over, will be poured into your lap. For with the measure you use, it will be measured to you. (Luke 6:38)*

Everything we have, is not really ours, but God's. He is the Creator of all things and therefore owns all things. What God wants from us is for us to be cheerful givers of a mere 10 percent of our resources, as a sign of faith.

How else will you, my fellow brothers and sisters in Christ, learn to experience the joy of God's provision if you will not test Him in this as He has asked us to do? I remember how scary it was to give a tenth of whatever monies came in during my first layoff. If you're like I was, 10 percent might as well be my life savings! However, I had been brought to a point in my life—a time where I was faced with making the decision to really and truly, once and for all, forever and ever, Amen—put my faith and trust in Christ. So I did.

I have learned from being faithful in tithing—no matter come what may—that God really does provide for us and meet our every need. I would not have been able to learn and embrace this truth, had I not done my part by stepping out in faith. I urge you, I beg you even, to give Him the opportunity to blow you away with His amazing power and love. You will not be disappointed, because you *can* trust God. He loves you more than you will ever know, my friend.

When we give God all that we have, He gives us all that *He* has.

> *No man should appear before the Lord empty-handed. Each of you must bring a gift in proportion to the way the Lord our God has blessed you. (Deuteronomy 16:16-17)*

> *Bring the whole tithe into the storehouse, that there may be food in my house. Test me in this, says the Lord Almighty, and see if I will not open the floodgates of Heaven and pour out so much blessing that you will not have room enough for it. (Malachi 3:10)*

Call Your Creditors

Next to filing for unemployment benefits, I think the second most important step you should take is that of calling your creditors to explain your situation and ask what, if anything, they can do to help cut payments during this season of your life.

Times are hard for just about everyone, and chances are the person answering the phone will be married to or know someone who has undergone a layoff, and as such will be compassionate toward you. All of my creditors but one were willing to give me a break by reducing my interest rate for several months.

If you are making car or house payments, ask if you can refinance your loans. Call your electricity provider and ask to be placed on balanced billing each month, if you have not already done so. Having a guaranteed set amount due each month for your utility bills will help you when it comes to establishing and maintaining a budget.

Financial/Credit Counseling

An evil man is trapped by his sinful talk, but a righteous man escapes trouble. (Proverbs 12:13)

Depending on your ability in the past to budget your money wisely, you might want to consider visiting a Christian financial planner or credit counselor for advice and to work up a livable budget for you.

"Consulting with a budget/debt counselor has advantages over trying to go through the period of unemployment alone, in that you have someone to encourage you in the 'trials,'" said Bill Buhl, director at Abundant Life Christian Credit Counseling. "A debt management program usually means lower interest rates, lower payments, and waiving of late and over-limit fees. All of these are helpful when you are trying to limit your money outflows. The counselor can give you ideas for spending less in many categories that you might not have thought about on your own," he added.

The top 10 steps a person should take immediately upon layoff, according to Buhl, are as follows:

1. Pray. Seek the Lord's help and guidance;
2. Establish a written budget (based on how you have been spending);
3. Radically reduce the amounts spent in each budget category that can be reduced;
4. List your assets (everything you own);
5. List your liabilities (everything you owe);
6. Avoid any new debt;
7. Establish a debt repayment plan;
8. Look for alternative sources of income, for you and for other family members;
9. Consider a radical change in your lifestyle, especially if the period of unemployment goes beyond three months; and
10. Do not give up!

Buhl recommends that a person who has been laid off take a home equity loan before drawing money from a 401K or IRA because as a loan, the home equity borrowed can be repaid.

"Taking money from the 401K or IRA is diminishing the funds one has in a tax deferred plan that is there for future years (for example, retiring)," he said. "The withdrawal also has current penalty tax consequences if the person is under fifty-nine and a half at the time of withdrawal, unless they set up a five-year stream of substantially equal payments."

Medical Insurance / COBRA

Many companies offer individuals an opportunity to buy COBRA insurance within thirty days of being laid off. I was shocked at the cost of COBRA insurance for my daughter and me—it was about $900 per month. Consider contacting your insurance agent to see what type of individual medical coverage is available and at what rates. For me, the price was too high.

If you decide as I did, that you cannot afford the luxury of medical insurance at any cost right now, what a great opportunity it is to trust in the Lord to meet all of your needs!

In the event that you require medical services, emergency room care, or a hospital stay, there are charity-based programs available at some facilities for people with little or no income. It is absolutely possible to get the care you need without having to worry about finances, but you do have to explain your situation and ask for assistance.

As an example, I required emergency room treatment twice for my accident, and my bill is currently under consideration to be released by way of the hospital's charity program. When I needed an MRI after it was determined that my leg fracture was not healing properly, my orthopedic surgeon negotiated with the facility on my behalf, reducing the cost of my bill from about $1,300 to $400. In addition, I was able to make payment arrangements of $20 per month, which was a great relief.

If you or any of your family members require medical attention, explain to your family doctor that you are laid off and without medical insurance, and ask if he or she can give you a reduced rate for an office visit. Our family doctor significantly reduced his rate for Emilie and me during this layoff, after I explained my situation. I didn't even ask him to do this—he did it on his own, in addition to giving me free sample medications in lieu of having to pay for prescription medication.

Unemployment Benefits and Taxes

While you are laid off, you should consider having federal taxes withheld from your unemployment check. Federal taxes are not withheld automatically so if you decide to do so, you must specifically request that they be taken out. While it is true that the amount of your unemployment checks will be reduced every two weeks, I learned to avoid a costly surprise when it came time to file my income taxes.

Taxpayer advocates are available for assistance if you are laid off and need guidance, by calling (877) 777-4778. In addition, the Volunteer Income Tax Assistance program provides trained volunteers by calling (800) 829-1040.

Ways to Cut Expenses

There are many ways to cut down on your living expenses while looking for work. Go ahead and get rid of cable TV and your newspaper subscription. If you have a computer, you can read the newspaper online.

Not being able to buy books right now is probably one of the hardest realities I have to face. I'm just as hungry as any lion in the proverbial den for good reading material! Nevertheless, the public library is available to everyone, so head on over there for a good book the next time you need a literary fix. Many libraries also offer free computer access, in addition to out of state newspapers (which means access to out of state job ads). Don't forget to keep track of your mileage if you're going to the library to use their computers for a job search.

Should you choose to keep your newspaper subscription, be sure to take advantage of the coupons found usually in the Sunday edition. Some might say that the money you save using coupons at the grocery store helps to balance out the cost of the monthly subscription for the newspaper that provided them to you. Coupons can be seductive, so make sure that you only use them for items you would normally buy. It doesn't make sense to save money on an item you don't normally use or need, just because you have a coupon for it. Also, take advantage of rebates offered by manufacturers by taking five minutes of your time to fill out the rebate form and placing it in the mail. Why would you *not* do this?!

I'm not sure how drug stores and department stores operate in your area, but where I live, many of them offer coupons for free gift cards valued at up to $25 if you purchase your new or transferred prescriptions from their pharmacies. If you're buying the medication anyway, why not get a gift card that you can turn around and use in the store and take advantage of their sale ads in the process?

Take advantage of a program that benefits consumers. Lest you think this is unethical, think again. It's all about marketing and competition. The stores that offer these programs are counting on your business and will pay you to give it to them. Nowhere in the coupon or in the store's policy does it state that the consumer *must* keep their prescription at that store for any length of time. It is a war between the competitors, with the consumer (for once) being the winner—providing you take advantage of it, that is.

There are many Internet websites that offer freebies. I didn't think they were legitimate until I started receiving items in the mail, including books, cosmetics, cleaning products, and more. Do a search for "free stuff" and be amazed. Why pay for things if you don't have to? I'm so serious—it really works, and it's fun to get free stuff in the mail!

If you have a computer, shop for the best Internet rates in your area. I was able to reduce the cost of my Internet service by $13 per month by changing service providers. Every dollar counts. Do I hear an "Amen"?!

If you are a single parent, inquire at your church if there are car ministries or home-repair programs available. Don't be afraid to network in your Bible study class for help.

If you use a cellular phone, since you probably won't be driving much until you find work, I would suggest that you call your coverage provider, explain that you are now unemployed, and ask them to put you on the least expensive plan available. They may give you what appears to be a low rate initially, but remember all of the taxes, fees, and the cost of the kitchen sink they throw in! When I negotiated rates with my cell phone service provider, I was able to get them down to $20 per month. They also gave me a two-month credit on my bill. Maybe it was my Southern belle charm, but I doubt it!

> *People who want to get rich fall into temptation and a trap and into many foolish and harmful desires that plunge men into ruin and destruction. For the love of money is a root of all kinds of evil. Some people, eager for money, have wandered from the faith and pierced themselves with many griefs. (1 Timothy 6:9-10)*

Bartering—It Works!

Learn to barter for the services you need, when at all possible. Currently I have a bartering program with Sherri, my friend, fellow church member, and hairdresser. Sherri provides hair-styling services, and I babysit her son in return. We each need and value what each of us brings to the table, we each get what we need, and neither of us spends a dime in the process.

During my first layoff, I had the joy of babysitting my niece while earning money. Pat and Martha were extremely generous with the hourly rate, but the greatest gift they gave me was not handing over a check, it was the ability to feel like I earned it. I felt like I was contributing instead of just taking, and this meant everything to me.

My friend Deb decided to be in charge of my entertainment during this layoff, and takes me to the movies in exchange for my helping her with a personal matter. Stella, another dear friend, paid my utility bills in exchange for my transporting her mom to and from physical rehab appointments after her mom had knee replacement surgery and for many months that followed.

Last year Emilie required some dental work that, even after insurance payments were applied, cost a great deal of money. I wrote a letter to my dentist, explained my situation, and asked if I could work off the balance on a part-time basis, a few hours a week, by answering the phones and/or doing other non-physical tasks. I was willing to pay off the balance, I told him, but could not afford to send much money each month under the current clear and present dangerous circumstances. He graciously offered a compromise by allowing me an opportunity to pay $20 per month without interest and without being reported to the credit bureau.

I also performed some public relations and marketing work for my orthopedic surgeon in exchange for several office visits. When he said he was surprised and "impressed" with my ingenuity and courage, I laughed it off and said I was doing what I needed to do to get the help I needed. It's all about survival!

Everyone has God-given skills and talents, including you. Think of the things you are good at and enjoy that may be of service to others who provide information or services that you need, and get busy with bartering. Not only will it save you money, it will give you something to do while waiting for your ship to roll in. Besides, it is a lot of fun!

The bottom line is, you have to ask for help if you need help. Sorry, I don't make the rules! And believe me, hard times like this call for us to do things we normally would never think of doing. By not seeking out help and getting creative in your ways of taking care of your needs, you are denying others the chance to show God's unconditional love for you. Why would you want to cheat God out of the chance to provide for you through others? Swallow that pride—its more expensive than you think, doesn't pay the bills or feed your family, and the taste of humble pie is surprisingly sweet.

For example, ten months after this current layoff, my accident, and still being unable to walk upright without pain, while talking to my sister Linda one day, a doctor she worked for asked her what was wrong. Linda apparently had tears in her eyes while on the phone with me explaining how difficult it was for me to walk even just a few steps. When we got off the phone, Linda explained my situation and within the next twenty-four hours, this doctor arranged with one of her peers to examine me at no cost. It was determined I needed knee surgery, and the doctor graciously agreed to perform it for only $500 after personally arranging with the hospital to discount its day rate by 50 percent. Both the doctor and hospital worked out payment arrangements with me.

My friend, I share this for two reasons.

First, I reiterate the importance of sharing your pain with those who love you. Allow them to minister to you on an emotional level. It is good for you and them because they know they are helping.

Second, you never know who God will work through to help you. Had I not given myself permission to unload some of my burden to Linda, the doctor would have never witnessed Linda's love for me and intervened.

CHAPTER SIX

Lessons From Layoff 101

Please take comfort in knowing that there are lessons you will learn during and after this layoff, just as there are blessings to be enjoyed both now and especially in the future. The key is to continue looking to and trusting God, always asking Him to help you to learn what it is He is trying to teach and develop whatever character trait He wants to develop.

By the way, I am well aware that I've been repeating myself. Maybe you're smarter than I am, but it took me a *long* time to really let go and trust God. I want to help you learn from the mistakes I've made so you can pole vault to the finish line of your layoff. Just trust God and be done with it already! Don't let this adversity go to waste—learn from it!

Lesson #1: God Provides

> Ask, and it will be given to you; seek, and you will find; knock, and the door will be opened to you. (Matthew 7:7)

Help for the Laid Off

One of the reasons God may have allowed or created this adversity in your life is to teach you that He is all you need in this life. To do this, God put you into a situation where you have no choice but to depend on Him to meet all your needs.

Once you humble yourself before Him and realize that the Creator of the universe is all you have, you will come to realize that He is all you need! God wants you to know, understand and accept that He truly is your source for everything, because He is.

You will learn that if you do your part by keeping your eyes on Him during your job search (and all other times, for that matter), God will do His part by providing for your needs both during your layoff and beyond.

The words of wisdom found in a poem titled "The Weaver" offer an explanation. According to the poet, once we are saved, God begins weaving together a new life for us, with fabrics and colors of His choosing. Our heavenly Father knows exactly what He wants it to look like, and how every stitch needs to be sewn. As humans, we are only able to see the backs of our respective tapestries, while God sees the front. The dark times of our lives represent the dark colors God uses, while the bright colors represent the good times. Only after we pass from this life to our eternal ones will God reveal the full and true glorious tapestries our lives represent by showing us the front side: the side He saw all along. Without dark times in our lives, we cannot appreciate those filled with light. It really is, that simple.

Lesson #2: Humble Pie

When pride comes, then comes disgrace, but with humility comes wisdom. (Proverbs 11:2)

Boy, it is difficult to ask for help, especially when one is used to being the sole (or at least equal) provider for the family. However, you will soon learn to eat humble pie by asking for and receiving the help you need. Thank God for the people He has placed in your life who you can go to. Thank God for the strangers who come into your life, give you what you need, and move on. You will learn that despite how you feel, you are not a charity case, and no one considers you to be a charity case. Who you are is someone who has been laid off due to downsizing or a reduction in workforce, through no fault of your own. Don't ever forget that your layoff is not a reflection of you or your job performance. It is an unfortunate circumstance in these troubling times we are facing while on Earth.

God is with you at all times. Although you cannot see Him, He is sitting right next to you, watching you read this book. Whether you believe me or not is irrelevant. It is true. His heart breaks when you're afraid to pick up the phone when it rings, and it isn't a job offer. The Lord is with you when your hand is out and money is placed into it. God knows our hearts and He gives us the strength, power, and humility we need to pick up the phone or write an email, asking for help—again. The people in your life know that you are not responsible for losing your job, and as such, you have nothing—not one thing—to be ashamed of.

Shortly after I was laid off this time, I spent $30 on a magnetic sign for my vehicle, which said, "Laid Off Editor Will Write for Money." It is silly, bold, and really fell in line with my sense of humor about the whole thing. If you can't laugh at yourself, please learn to do so! I received many phone calls from people on the road, and it was a great way to share my story with them. You never know who knows whom. Has it led to work? Not yet, but it might. Do I care what people think when they see the sign? Not one bit. God's opinion matters most to me.

Lesson #3: The Dangers of Making Assumptions

As for God, His way is perfect, the Word of the Lord is flawless. (Psalm 18:30)

Whoever advised, "Don't count your chickens until they hatch" was a very wise person. I know I learned the hard way, not to talk as though I have a job offer when in fact, I don't. Learn through my mistake the dangers of making assumptions about a possible job. You do not want to be jilted at the job altar, trust me. Let me explain.

A few months ago, I was rejected for a dream job that I was *convinced* was God's will for me. I was, in fact, *so* convinced that I had contacted a number of businesses in a city about a thousand miles from my home concerning demographical information, apartment locating, etc., to start getting things lined up. Imagine how hard—and humbling—it was for me a few days after receiving the rejection notice to receive the information package from the city's chamber of commerce that contained information about where I *thought* I was moving to.

I wailed, moaned, and groaned for several days, even though I know that God is in control and there is a lesson to be learned or a character trait He is trying to develop as a result of this emotional trauma. "Lord, I feel like I have enough character to stage a Broadway play already. What have I done to deserve this? Did I talk about it too much out of excitement, and jinx myself? Did I somehow sound prideful over the thought of working for you in a full-time ministerial position? What?" I asked.

After talking with my brother, Pat, I realized it was not God's will for me to sell my house and relocate across the country to take a position paying considerably less than what I was making at my previous full-time position. I was willing to do it, because I felt it was an opportunity to step out in faith like Christ asks us to do.

My brother also said he believed this opportunity was from Satan rather than from God, as a way to bring me down and lose everything I have. I never thought about it this way, but I have come to the conclusion that he was right. You see, the rejection happened *within hours* after I had prayed for God to "shut the door on this opportunity" if it was not His will for my life. God not only shut the door, He slammed it tight! And I know Him well enough to fall to my knees with thanks for doing so, even though I do not understand it and even though it hurt.

All of my sisters comforted me by defending my beliefs and actions, saying that I was not being proud or arrogant, that I had every right, based on the interview, the fact that I was qualified for the job, etc., to believe it was mine, and that I was just excited. Of course, my mother wanted to call the employer up and give him a peace of her mind for leading me on a wild goose chase. *Boy,* was she mad! Hell hath no fury like a mother when her child is hurting!

Lesson #4: Jesus—Not Junk—Is the Source of Your Joy

> *Do not love the world or anything in the world. If anyone loves the world, the love of the Father is not in him. For everything in the world—the cravings of sinful man, the lust of his eyes and the boasting of what he has and does—comes not from the Father but from the world. The world and its desires pass away, but the man who does the will of God lives forever. (1 John 2:15-17)*

Enduring a layoff and learning to do without certain "things" will help you understand and accept that Jesus is the source of your joy, peace, and strength. Feelings like these cannot be bought at any price, at any store. You do not need fancy clothes or the latest gadgets around the house, nor do you need the latest version of software or digital anything. Believe it or not, you can still get to the grocery store in a used car—you do not have to have a new one. Honest. The planet will not melt if you have to watch movies on a VCR rather than a DVD player. Try it and see for yourself! You and I may *want* these things, but we do not *need* these things.

Learning to live without the "finer things in life" during a layoff is one of those character-building experiences designed to show that you will, in fact, survive without them. Try reading a wonderful book, *The Search for Significance* by Robert S. McGee, when you have time.

Let me ask you something.

Who cares about you more: God, or the people who create clever advertising designed to play on your insecurities by persuading you that you're somehow less valuable of a human being unless you buy their products—with money you don't have?

While it is true they are only doing their jobs—and I don't begrudge anyone who makes an honest living—the point is your life is no better or worse, and you are no more valuable to anyone if you do or do not use or buy whatever it is the world is selling. Only Jesus Christ loves you unconditionally and without fault, so why not focus on pleasing Him instead of others?

Surviving a layoff will show you what you can and cannot live without. God promises to meet all of your needs, and He will. You will have food, clothing and shelter—the things you need for survival. Think of what a lean, mean, witnessing machine you will be once this phase of your life is over!

God never promised us, nor does He owe us, a rose garden. If God gave us everything we wanted, when we wanted it, and how we wanted it, we'd probably all be dead by now. Add to that, there would be no reason to seek His face and His glory, there would be no eternal life to look forward to in Heaven. God is not some cosmic spiritual vending machine. He created us to glorify Him, not the other way around! God owes us nothing, and we owe Him everything!

Lesson #5: How Strong is Your Marriage?

Years ago there was a song by Willie Nelson and Waylon Jennings that spoke about walking away from "the high life" and getting back to the basics of love. Good song, great message.

One thing is for sure: If you are married, a layoff will prove the mettle of your marriage. My hope and prayer is that your spouse meant the words, "for better or worse, for richer or poorer," and married you for *who you are* rather than the lifestyle your former income provided. What better way to reconnect with your God and your spouse than to begin and end each day on your knees together in prayer before the Lord?

Use this layoff experience to strengthen your marriage and your relationship with God. If you are having a bad day and need encouragement, tell your spouse. God knows what you need and how you feel, but your spouse won't unless you talk!

Lesson #6: The Importance of Being Debt-Free

> *Keep your lives free from the love of money and be content with what you have, because God has said, Never will I leave you; never will I forsake you. (Hebrews 13:5)*

There is nothing like learning to make ends meet without a regular source of sufficient income being earned to learn why it is so important to live within our means and become debt-free. I'm sure you'll agree with me when I say that enduring one layoff per lifetime is enough! The reality is that we may face another layoff in the future. What better time than *now* to get your bills paid off as soon as possible after you get hired into your new position.

You will learn that money most definitely does not buy happiness and that credit cards are *not* your friends. Perhaps this experience was the kick-start you needed to get all things financial out on the table. And, you will learn to get back to the very simple basic pleasures of life. Now more than ever, you will learn that the best things in life aren't things at all, and that the best things in life are free.

Lesson #7: Your Children *Will* Survive!
One day, months and years from now when this nightmare has ended, your children will have benefited from this layoff in ways you cannot imagine. How you respond to this layoff is critical for the sake and well-being of your kids, for you are teaching them life skills at all times. They are watching you, listening to you, and living through this experience with you. "Do Mom and Dad *really* trust God?" they may be asking themselves, depending on how old they are.

"I don't think any parent can hold it together all the time in front of their kids, or that it is healthy to act as though they are," said Katherine Moore, Christian Counseling Associates. "Teaching a child to cope with circumstances in life can't be done in a void. The lesson comes from how a parent deals with explaining to the child after they have 'lost it.' I think a parent should give the child the opportunity to ask questions and for the parent to answer those questions truthfully as much as possible.

"Kids will fill in the blanks if they aren't filled in by the parent, and it is naïve to think they don't sense something is going on. Kids don't need details. Probably the best thing for them to know is that a parent has a support system, and that is the most vital thing for the parent, too," Moore added.

Together, Emilie and I learned the fine art of humility, the kindness and generosity of strangers, and that God always provides for His children, no matter what.

As an example, my family rarely celebrates Thanksgiving together because it is just so hard to coordinate our schedules. During my first layoff, years ago, it looked as though we were going to have cereal or beans and cornbread again. *Again.* Imagine my surprise when there was a knock on the door one night, and in walked a woman and four teenagers—none of them I had ever met before—carrying grocery bags filled with a turkey, vegetables, dressing, pies, and everything I would need to make and experience a real Thanksgiving for us. Do you want to try and tell me there is not a God of this universe who loves and cares for me deeply? That same wonderful Abba Father loves and cares for you too. Believe it.

Weeks passed, seasons changed, and still I was unable to get work. We had been down to the bare essentials for so long. We had taken so much for granted and now were beginning to learn that we could, in fact, live without a daily newspaper, cable TV, and computer of our own, among other things.

Oh, how I longed to give her more. Oh, how I cried over not being able to take Emilie to a movie now and then. "God, she is only nine years old, why does she have to suffer so much at such a young age?" I cried.

Instead of relying on what money can buy, Emilie and I grew stronger and closer together through this experience and became actively involved in our church. Church became our social life, and I couldn't think of anywhere I'd rather be.

Over the years, Emilie has seen time and time again how God answers prayers. "I definitely learned the value of a dollar, and that I can live and be happy without a lot of material things," she told me. "As my mom, you taught me to trust in God for all things, at all times, and to never be too proud to ask for and receive help. Everyone needs a hand at some point in life," she concluded.

I feel this bears repeating: As difficult as this may be to accept and believe, your kids *will* survive this experience with you, and come out better for having done so. It is okay for your kids to see you on down days, but critical for their spiritual growth to witness you reading your Bible and remaining actively involved with your church.

Each time the Lord provides for your every need, be sure and point out to your kids that God has "done it again." Make the best use of your time together without all of the extras that money can provide. Learn to talk to your kids, and get to know them for the first time, if that's the case. Get them outside with you when you go for physical exercise, and let them pray with you each night. Play board games or read books aloud to each other.

"When the Lord is working in your life and has allowed you to endure a layoff, it may be happening for the very reason to let your children know you don't walk through life with a silver spoon in your mouth. There are bottoms you hit, and when you hit rock-bottom the only way to look is up toward the Lord," explained Gayle Ramin, a licensed Bible therapist and certified Christian counselor.

Lesson #8: Faith That Leaps, Reaps

I believe one of the things God rejoices in most, other than when a child of His accepts His free gift of salvation, is when one of us goes spiritually silly and takes an enormous leap of faith. One thing about a layoff is true: It will give you faith whether you want it or not. And, if you're lucky, once—just once during this layoff— you may be at the end of your rope and do something totally wild, trusting God at His Word, and going for the unknown, whatever that may be. Allow me to share with you how God rewarded me for the leap of faith I took during my first layoff.

Back then, Emilie and I lived in the cheapest apartment I could find. Never did the phrase "you get what you pay for" come into play as prominently as it did back then. Summer heat in Houston is not to be believed, and in August 1996, my landlord informed me that I would be charged $50 each time I called for service on the air conditioner, which had broken seven times over the summer. I was so angry and hot that I packed Emilie up, and we went to the nearest Hotel Joe I could find so we could have at least *one* night with air conditioning like normal people. People with jobs.

We opened the door to that room, threw our suitcases on the floor, and jumped on the beds for ten minutes at least, squealing like stuck pigs because we had *air conditioning!* For one night, after we took our showers, we would not dry off only to begin sweating before we ever lay down to sleep. Yippee!

The following morning, my mind continued to be clearly lost, because I treated us to—get this—*breakfast* at Hotel Joe. Like normal people. Like people on vacation. Like people with jobs.

The minute I opened the door to my blistering apartment that afternoon, a tired, brittle twig in my mind snapped once and for all. "God does not want us living this way, and we are *out of here*. I don't care what happens, I don't care what I have to do, I don't care that I don't have a permanent job, I don't care that I can't afford it, I don't care about anything, Mister, just get me out of here." So I did. I hit the road, Jack, and I never looked back. Not once.

> *I tell you the truth, if you have faith as small as a mustard seed, you can say to this mountain, Move from here to there' and it will move. Nothing will be impossible for you. (Matthew 17:20)*

After dropping our overnight bag on the floor of our apartment and taking Emilie to a friend's house, I began visiting apartment complexes in the area. Hell hath no fury like a woman whose mind has been broken from stress! I put a deposit down on a new apartment, turned in my notice to the landlord, and began packing that very afternoon. I had, in fact, purposely and intentionally increased my rent by $300 a month without a permanent job in site. Clearly the heat and humidity had fried my brain!

At the time, I was working as a contract employee as a secretary for a nearby company. While I had worked there for several months, there had been no mention of the job going permanent. Still, I did not care. Even if we could not pay rent after thirty days of living in the new apartment, I did not care. I did not care if I lived, I did not care if I died. All I cared about was getting out of that dump we were living in. A voice inside me—that I now know was that of the Holy Spirit—said "scoot," and so we did.

In October 1996, only two months after taking that leap of faith, a miracle happened. I followed the advice found in Matthew 7:7-8: "Ask and it will be given to you; seek and you will find; knock and the door will be opened to you. For everyone who asks, receives; he who seeks finds; and to him who knocks, the door will be opened."

I accepted an offer for my first full-time editorial position and have never looked back.

Lesson #9: Be Bold and Courageous!

Now is not the time to be timid, my friend. In fact, now is time to try something you've never done before. Follow your dreams. I know you have them, so go for it! God has given you this season of your life for many reasons, and one of them may be to give you time to reach for the stars and see what happens.

As an example, I was a secretary for over twenty years who only dreamed of writing full time for a living. Without a college degree or formal training of any kind, I came to the realization that if I didn't step out and do something—anything—my dreams for sure wouldn't become reality.

With the boldness and determination God gave me, I made the ridiculous move of calling an editor of the *Houston Chronicle* back in 1992. I introduced myself and explained my situation, and asked if I could write just one article for her. "If you like it, great; if you don't, you'll never hear from me again. But please, won't you just give me this chance so I can see if I have what it takes?" Lo and behold, she said, "Okay."

I wrote the article, she used it and immediately gave me another writing assignment. You cannot know how thrilling it was seeing my name in print for the first time and getting paid for it! I continued writing for the paper for another year before becoming bold again, this time approaching magazines about freelance writing. Doors opened and I soon found myself writing for up to eight magazines at a time.

When I was laid off from my secretarial position in 1994, it was as if God was challenging me, "How bad do you want to write full time?" I had more time to write more articles, developing and strengthening myself with each assignment. In 1995, after a year of being without full-time work, I challenged myself to try and go after the oil and gas industry publications, a field I knew absolutely nothing about.

I called all of the energy publications I could find in Houston, inquiring about freelancers. One of the editors I spoke with said they weren't looking for any at that time but encouraged me to send my resume and clips just the same. So I did.

God's wonders never cease, because exactly one year later that editor's position became available. Not only did the Lord bless me with a full-time job, He fulfilled my dream of writing full time for a living! (See Lesson #8, when I took my leap of faith.) I laugh in amazement, remembering how worried I was about taking the job. The president of the company I had been working for suddenly made me a relatively decent offer for full-time work, and I had to choose between the security of knowing I could do the job and facing the challenge of proving to myself and others that I could, in fact, make the career switch and go for my dreams. Satan really did a number on my head at the time, as I was so afraid of failing. Yet, God helped me overcome my fear and go for it.

I am challenging you to be bold and courageous, especially if you don't feel like doing so. If my own experiences aren't evidence enough of what God can do with a person despite a lack of a formal college education or training of any type, let's look at young David in the Old Testament.

When David was a young shepherd boy tending his flock in the fields, there came a time when an enormous giant named Goliath was terrorizing Saul and the men of Israel day in and day out. The dude was like 10 feet tall and sported a heavy bronze helmet and full-scale armor. The spear he carried weighed 600 shekels of iron, and a shield protected him as he stood there.

Every day Goliath would come down into the valley and shout at the top of his lungs:

> *Why do you come out and line up for battle? Am I not a Philistine, and are you not the servants of Saul? Choose a man and have him come down to me. If he is able to fight and kill me, we will become your subjects; but if I overcome him and kill him, you will become our subjects and serve us.* (1 Samuel 17:8-9)

No one—not even Saul himself—was willing to take him on. In walks David from the fields and, immediately upon learning of the challenge, he was like, "piece of cake." David told Saul he was able to kill Goliath, but Saul basically said, "No way, you're just a wimpy kid." David, knowing the Lord God was on his side, entered into a debate with Saul, telling him how while he was tending sheep in the fields, he killed both lions and bears. Saul finally agreed to let David go for it but made him wear Saul's own garments and bronze helmet. Obviously, Saul was skeptical about David's faith in his abilities.

David began to move forward but found himself weighted down with this heavy outfit and quickly took it off. He strolled into the field to face Goliath with five smooth stones and a sling. And, with one sling of the stone, Goliath fell to the ground, a dead man.

What does this say to you? What it says to me, is that in order for God to do great things for us, we have to believe that He will, in fact, help us. We have to believe in ourselves enough, believe in our God-given dreams enough, to go for it! I have made a lot of mistakes in my life, but I believe God uses me anyway because He sees that if nothing else, I am bold enough to believe His promise that I can, in fact, do all things through Christ, who strengthens me (Philippians 4:13).

The Lord is working in your life and in the lives of your family and friends through this experience. He could be equipping you for future service, making you strong in your faith so that you will be able to witness to and minister to those He places in your life at some point in the future, who are without faith, hope, and love. But you must remain alert and attentive to His voice.

Listen!

CHAPTER SEVEN

Layoffs Produce an Abundance of Fruitful Blessings

But the fruit of the Spirit is love, joy, peace, patience, kindness, goodness, faithfulness, gentleness, and self-control...
Galatians 5:22-23

Although it may be hard for you to believe at this time, you and I are each receiving enormous gifts through enduring our layoff experiences. The blessings you receive may be one and the same as those I have been given, or they may be different, depending upon where you are in your walk with the Lord. However, the greatest of all these is the free gift of salvation.

My friend, we are called to love God no matter what, whether we receive benefits by being obedient to Him or not. God has already given us the best gift we could ever have at no cost to us but at an enormous price to Him, by sacrificing His only begotten Son, Jesus Christ, on the Cross to pay for our sins—past, present, and future.

You cannot ask for more than that.

Life on this earth is but a blink of the eye. The *real* life is our eternal one in Heaven, where Jesus has gone to prepare a place for us.

We may never know what higher purposes God has in mind for us at the end of our respective tunnels, and all of us need to be okay with that. After all, God owes us nothing, we owe Him everything. We must strive for complete obedience at all times, to the best of our human abilities. If we learn to and continue to trust in Him at all times and rest in His everlasting arms, both now during this phase of our lives and also in the future, He promises to meet our every need. He already is.

You and I will find jobs again. We *will* be able to once again provide for ourselves and our families. Our respective layoffs will *not* last forever. I know this from experience, and I hope you will believe me. Do not forget that today—as I write this chapter—I have $4.64 in my checking account; however, my bills are paid to date, there is food in my kitchen, my daughter and I have clothes to wear, and a roof over our heads. Be grateful for your health, if you have it. Be thankful for your family and friends, too.

"I wonder what would happen if tomorrow morning we woke up with only the things we had thanked God for the day before," a pastor once said.

Do I sound stressed out? I hope not, because I am filled with joy and excitement as I write this, knowing that God is working in my life and yours at this very moment. You *never know* what will happen in the course of a few hours or a day! It is just a matter of time before you receive a job offer and I, as well.

Love

Who shall separate us from the love of Christ? (Romans 8:35)

Chances are, you are feeling love from all directions during this temporary phase of your life. At least, that is my prayer for you. I suspect you are seeing first-hand, God's faithful and provisional love through the emotional, physical, spiritual, and financial support of the friends, family, and even strangers who He has placed in your life. There is no question in my mind that there are, indeed, angels among us. Don't take my word for it—let's look at what the writer of Hebrews 1:14 says: "Are not all angels ministering spirits sent to serve those who will inherit salvation?" Remember the story I previously shared about the doctor who overheard my conversation with Linda? That woman was an angel if I ever met one.

Perhaps you are from a family that has never been close in the past, and your family has risen to the occasion during this crisis time in your life to help you. What a wonderful side effect from this pain! Maybe everyone in your life has been too busy "chasing the wind" to realize that what's most important in life is following God's commandment to love one another as Christ has loved us. God may have used this layoff experience in your life to draw your family and friends closer together, strengthen your marriage, get rid of idols in your life—there are infinite reasons as to why this has happened to us.

Ask yourself, "Are my needs being met? Do I feel loved for the first time in a long time?" Have you been ministered to by an angel you've never met? Open your eyes. If it hasn't happened yet, it will. Why? Because God loves you more than any of us could ever fathom.

> *For I am convinced that neither death nor life, neither angels nor demons, neither the present nor the future, nor any powers, neither height nor depth, nor anything else in all creation, will be able to separate us from the love of God that is in Christ Jesus our Lord. (Romans 8:38-39)*

Joy

The joy of the Lord, truly is our strength and what a blessing this is! One day you will have the joy of knowing that based on this layoff experience, everything God says and promises in His Word is true. You will learn that there is no need to fear, worry, or have doubts about whether God loves you and will provide for you. As a result, you will have true inner joy that can only come from surviving the winds of adversity with Jesus by your side. Nothing compares or even comes close to the indescribable peace and joy of having a relationship with Jesus Christ, and it is only when you have this relationship that you will understand how I can profess this. And, no person on this Earth will ever love you as unconditionally and completely as Jesus Christ. No one.

Whatever you do not have, ask God for it in faith and He will give it to you, as long as it is in accordance with His will for your life. Jesus says in John 15:7-8: "If you remain in me and my words remain in you, ask whatever you wish, and it will be given you. This is to my Father's glory, that you bear much fruit, showing yourselves to be my disciples."

Which brings me to another point: As you are walking this path and once you have been given gainful employment, you (and I) are called to share with others the goodness and love of God that has been shown to us through others. We are called to be witnesses of Christ's provisions at all times. How else can we encourage and uplift one another, if not by sharing experiences and lessons learned first-hand?

Peace

Yet if you devote your heart to him and stretch out your hands to him, if you put away the sin that is in your hand and allow no evil to dwell in your tent, then you will lift up your face without shame; you will stand firm and without fear. You will surely forget your trouble, recalling it only as waters gone by. Life will be brighter than noonday, and darkness will become like morning. You will be secure, because there is hope; you will look about you and take rest in your safety. You will lie down, with no one to make you afraid, and many will court your favor. (Job 11:13-19)

I suspect that you will receive the peace that only a personal relationship with Jesus Christ can bring, as I have. You may feel at times like you are walking on a tightrope with your children in your arms, flames rising up all around you. Keep your eyes on Jesus. Do not be like Peter, who at once began walking on the water toward Jesus but began to drown the minute he took his eyes off Him. You know the story:

> *During the fourth watch of the night Jesus went out to them, walking on the lake. When the disciples saw him walking on the lake, they were terrified. "It's a ghost," they said, and cried out in fear. But Jesus immediately said to them: "Take courage! It is I. Do not be afraid." "Lord, if it's you," Peter replied, "tell me to come to you on the water." "Come," He said. Then Peter got down out of the boat, walked on the water and came toward Jesus. But when he saw the wind, he was afraid and, beginning to sink, cried out, "Lord, save me!" Immediately Jesus reached out his hand and caught him. "You of little faith," He said, "why did you doubt?" (Matthew 14:25-31)*

No one knows better than me how easy it is to succumb to fear now and then, especially during a layoff. My friend, the only way you can have the peace you need is to know, accept and understand that it is yours for the asking. Don't let Satan steal your joy and rob you of what he once had but threw away. Satan will do everything in his power to bring you down and keep you down. The battle has already been won, and the good news is God wins!

Shortly before His death by crucifixion, Jesus explained to His disciples that upon His death, God would send the Counselor—the Holy Spirit—to them and all believers to guide and protect us for the rest of our lives. Because God is true to His word, we now have the peace that surpasses all understanding. Jesus says, "Peace I leave with you; my peace I give you. I do not give to you as the world gives. Do not let your hearts be troubled and do not be afraid" (John 14:27).

If losing my job, falling 16 feet out of a tree and breaking myself in the process, walking around for nearly a year before learning I needed knee surgery, and worrying on an almost daily basis about a terminally ill friend committing suicide weren't enough to deal with, my mom recently passed away unexpectedly, needlessly and in a horrific manner. I remember driving nearly an hour each way to and from the hospital, using a crutch for the gas pedal (because of my messed-up knee).

Only God knows what is next on His agenda for my life, and I embrace whatever future calamities may come, because I know He has a good purpose for them and I know this time of trial will not last forever. Nor will yours.

While many people may believe I have many reasons to succumb to paralyzing fear, I have complete peace, instead. How is this possible? God is answering countless prayers that are being offered by my treasured collection of dear, personal friends as well as those friends and pastors from my church family. What a blessing it is to know that people are praying for you at all times.

Patience and Perseverance

Ah, patience and perseverance. The "P" words. Enduring a layoff is one of the most effective ways of gaining patience and learning how to persevere that I know of, because you have no choice but to do what you can to find employment and in the process, learn patience by waiting upon the Lord. Now you *could* take matters into your own hands and perhaps accept the first job that's offered—but is that wise to do? How do you know if that is the right job for you without consulting God first?

Imagine what would have happened had I not prayed to God and asked Him to shut the door on that first job opportunity—the one I wanted so much and was so convinced was mine because it was a ministerial position? Had I not sought God's advice, I believe that I would have accepted that job, sold my house, and moved to a city far, far away for a position that may or may not have lasted, because it wasn't God's best choice for me.

Sure, of course I was devastated because I can think of nothing I would rather do than work for the Lord full time, especially since He is my Divine Employer and yours! You *bet* I cried like a baby to God, pouting and licking my wounds. I was pitiful for about two days. After much prayer and contemplation, I received what I asked for—the ability to "get over it" and get on with the process of living, loving, and looking upward until my proverbial ship comes in. And, in the process of doing so, I am gaining patience.

No matter how rough the road is and how scary it is to be in a dark closet right now, I have learned that I am capable of persevering through this experience not once, but twice. In a distorted sort of way, I take great pleasure in knowing that I can do without many things that the world has to offer, because when your back is up against the wall, it's amazing what you can learn to live without. Surviving something like a layoff shows what you are made of. I am fearfully and wonderfully made by God, and so are you!

I consider myself honored and humbled to be in this situation again because I learned from the first layoff experience that God uses all pain for His glory and to the good of all who love Him, just as He has promised. In the book of Romans, the Apostle Paul writes that we should rejoice in our sufferings.

> *Not only so, but we also rejoice in our sufferings, because we know that suffering produces perseverance; perseverance, character; and character, hope. (Romans 5:3-4)*

> *Consider it pure joy, my brothers, whenever you face trials of many kinds, because you know that the testing of your faith develops perseverance. Perseverance must finish its work so that you may be mature and complete, not lacking anything. (James 1:2-4)*

Kindness, Goodness, and Gentleness

Open your eyes to see the kindness, goodness, and gentleness of those you know, and even some you don't. The ways that God speaks to His children most often are through His Word, through your circumstances, and through other believers. Perhaps someone will help you in an unusually creative way, at a time when you need it most. By witnessing and receiving caring words of comfort or a hug when it becomes hard to breathe because you may be crying so hard, you, in turn, will be able to one day return these blessings to others whom God will place in your path. Other than to glorify God, this is what life's all about.

My life is filled with good, kind, and gentle souls, and I hope and pray that yours is as well. If you are lonely, reach out and connect with your church family during this time. If you do not have one, what better time to start visiting area churches and get involved? Let people love you as Christ loves you. And then, once you have received the love of God through His work in others, praise Him and get the word out to others about the power and glory of His name! Part of being forced to endure trials of any nature, is developing humility and placing yourself in line to receive comfort, strength, and restoration through the body of Christ. You are only hurting yourself if you continue to rely solely on yourself.

Faithfulness

The words of the song, "Great is thy Faithfulness," ring true during times like these. There *is* no shadow of turning with Him. All I have needed, His hands *have* provided. God is true, trustworthy and faithful above all else. "Be still and know that I am God," David writes in Psalm 46:10. God has been faithful to me by providing for my needs as He is to you by taking care of you, as well.

One day you will be able to speak from experience, as a true follower of Jesus Christ, the wonderfulness of who He is. You cannot say you know something works unless you do. Witnessing to others about the love of God and how He has worked miracles in your life cannot be done unless you yourself have seen first-hand that of which you speak. There is no testimony without a test.

My faith was really struck by the lightning of Almighty God shortly after my first layoff experience ended. It wasn't until it was all over with, that I could look back as David and many others in the Bible did, and see how God's hand was with me all along. I learned first-hand the benefits of being obedient to the best of my ability. And, I was rewarded for my faithfulness in a multitude of ways. What a blessing, to be used by the Lord! The time is coming when you will also be able to share with hurting people how God has been so faithful to provide, comfort, protect, and guide you.

Self-Control
To be honest, self-control is something I continue to struggle with because, for me, it is very hard to get a hold of. I have gone through phases where I have great self-control and others when I have failed miserably. Like the Apostle Paul, who suffered with a "thorn in his side," having the ability to say "no" to fleshly desires does not come easily to me.

I confess that I *do* enjoy some of the things of this world, like good books, great food, traveling, quality electronics, going to the movies, live theatre, and being able to buy new CDs. The library feeds my need to read, and I am able to still enjoy live theatre by volunteering as an usher at the Alley Theatre. Although Emilie and I cannot afford to do many activities we enjoy right now, it certainly isn't the end of the world, is it?

Focus on how you're able to spend more time with your family and be grateful for all you do have.

Without a source of regular income, you will be blessed with the ability to rely on Jesus for the self-control you need. Just like the Apostle Paul, you and I can be strong, even though we are weak, through the awesome and almighty power of Jesus Christ.

The Bottom Line

No matter who you were when you took your first step down this path, you will walk away from it at the end as a stronger, more compassionate, wiser, and more generous person. You will be equipped to minister to others God will place in your path who have lost their jobs. I know, as do you, this road we are on is a difficult one.

I hate it, if you really want to know the truth.

At the same time, however, I know—I know that I know that I know that I *know*—that God is God, I am not, and He has a good plan for my life and a good reason for my suffering and humiliation at having to accept help from family, friends, and strangers over and over again. I may not ever know the reason, and I have learned to be okay with that, as well. God loves me, I love Him, and that is that.

In addition to the blessings you will receive from losing your job, your family and friends have a chance to be obedient before the Lord by helping you with a cheerful heart. I don't know about you, but it helps me to accept painful situations if I think these experiences may be able to be used by God for the greater good of everyone by pointing our hearts towards Him and Him alone.

Chapter Eight

Encourage Your Discouraged

If anyone does not provide for his relatives, and especially for his immediate family, he has denied the faith and is worse than the unbeliever.
1 Timothy 5:8

If your loved one is laid off and you are not sure how to treat them (what to do and not do, say and not say), then this chapter is for you.

The loss of a job is devastating, not just to the individual now faced without a way of earning income, but also to those around that person, regardless of the relationship. Whether it is your husband or your wife, sister or brother, son or daughter, mother or father and yes, even friend—when one person is laid off, many people are affected. Without having experienced it yourself personally, you *cannot know* how it feels to walk in our broken shoes. You probably find it hard to understand the mood swings, depression, insomnia, and forgetfulness.

Help for the Laid Off

Walk a Mile in Our Shoes

Being laid off is like walking through a minefield or hopping from one lily pad to the next, afraid of falling. Don't like this scenario? How about imagining you're carrying your child or children in your arms while walking a tight rope with your bare feet, underneath you is fire or snakes or whatever it is you're afraid of. Sometimes you can sense God's presence and sometimes you can't, but you have to trust that He is there—because He is.

Your loved one has quite enough to do with respect to looking for work and maintaining their sanity without having to worry about how they're going to make ends meet. It would be unbelievably helpful for the person to know what he can and cannot count on each month. Those in my family who were in a position to help divided the amount I needed each month to live on between them. I did not have to ask them for help every month: They knew I needed it, and they stepped up to the plate.

Every day that your loved one and I are unable to work at gainful employment is another day we are unable to contribute to some sort of retirement program. If anything, the more time that passes, the closer the day is coming where we may have to cash out what little retirement savings we have to live. I already have. My heart hurts for those who do not even have this to fall back on. Please be aware that in addition to being concerned about our present circumstances, in the back of our minds we are also wondering about our future circumstances. That's a lot to process, people.

There are days when the one you love may not want to take a shower or even change out of their pajamas. Depression does that to people. Your loved one needs unconditional love and support now more than ever. They need to be listened to, heard, validated, and affirmed that they are still as valuable to you today as they ever were, with or without a job. Call them once in a while. Don't assume someone else is doing so.

You would be surprised how loud, silence can be.

Being laid off, especially through no fault of your own, can be a very humiliating, emotionally debilitating experience, especially if it lasts a long time.

"You must remember this person is feeling very bad about themselves. They've lost the opportunity to help their family. Many women lose respect for their husbands when they lose their job, because suddenly they're being a stay-at-home parent," explained Christian counselor Gayle Ramin. "She needs to thank God and her husband she has someone there to look after her children if she has a job outside the home."

Knowing there are hundreds of people applying for the same position is very hard to accept, yet we who are without work must continue to try. What does it feel like? Imagine you're in a completely dark bottomless pit, and each day you begin climbing a ladder, reaching for rungs you cannot see. You're doing everything you can not to slip and fall. On most days when you reach, you find there is no other rung to grab a hold of; for example, there are no more jobs to apply for that day.

When you get any interest from a prospective employer, any crumb at all, you begin to climb faster and if you squint your eyes, you swear you're seeing the light of day. When an interview is not offered, or worse, it goes forward but then a rejection letter is received, it's like someone has kicked your hands off the ladder's rung and as you slide down the ladder once again, your heart, mind, and soul absorb more splinters than before. It's like the world is saying, "Go back to your hole where you belong. You're not good enough." Your house is on fire, your children (who you're supposed to protect and provide for) are inside, and where are you? In the fires of unemployment hell.

Accepting financial help is one of the hardest things an unemployed person has to do. Please don't add an emotional price tag to go along with it.

I know in my own experience, when I am having a really hard day of discouragement, Satan has an absolute circus in my mind. My family would be shocked to know sometimes I think they believe I'm kicking back, "working the system," and living the good life while they help support me. "Why do I think this?" I wonder. No one has said or even remotely implied as such, so it must be one of two things: 1.) this layoff and the length of time I am suffering with repeated rejection is starting to get to me, or 2.) Satan is having a field day in my mind. Without the benefit of talking to a pastor, who can quickly point out that this is clearly a Satanic attack, I would not be able to snap out of this wrong thinking.

And you know what? These thoughts are harder to accept then checks from family members, because if it were true, it meant they lost respect for me as a person, a family member, and a professional. Would they react differently if they were in my shoes? Did I ever ask God to allow me to suffer like this, not once but *twice*? No.

But remember, it's not about me, and it's not about you, either. Enduring a layoff, like many other life trials, is about letting God be God in our lives. I do not know what the purpose of being laid off twice is, but I accept it because I know—I *know*—He loves me more than anyone else loves me.

What to Say, What Not to Say

> *An anxious heart weighs a man down, but a kind word cheers him up. (Proverbs 12:25)*

When talking to your loved one—whether through a phone call, email, letter, or personal visit—I recommend letting them be the one to bring up the job search, job market, etc. In many ways, layoff victims are grieving in ways that are similar to the loss of a loved one. While the object or subject of the loss is different, loss is loss, and it hurts. And, it can be especially scary when not only your life is depending on it, but the lives of your family are depending as well.

If the person does bring up the issue, make sure you give them your undivided attention, and affirm them with statements like, "You sure are working hard at finding work," and "You're doing everything you can; I don't know that I could hold out as long or as well as you." People who have lost their jobs want and need to be treated as normally as possible. If you want to help anonymously, send a gift card from a local store with no return address. One of the nicest things someone did for me was sending movie passes to Emilie and me. For two hours one afternoon we were able to be "normal" people and forget about our circumstances.

"It is very important for spouses to reaffirm their loved one, and tell them their self-worth is not based on their jobs—that is not who they are," Ramin said. "We need to remember that it could have happened to us, and what would you want from me if I had been laid off? I would want you to be supportive of me, treat and talk to me with respect, and not speak condescendingly. People have to make sacrifices. When we're in a marriage or any type of relationship, it is about sacrificing our needs and placing the needs of others above all else."

Much of how adult children respond to their parent's layoff depends on how they were raised, Ramin continued. "Were they shown affection and support during their bad times, by their parents? If they were, they will understand their parents are going through a crisis and try to help them in any way they can. If adult children were raised by strict parents who never expressed love and compassion, they will more than likely respond to their parents in this same manner." While that may be understandable, it doesn't make it okay.

Whenever you talk to your loved one and they are crying, whatever you do, do *not* tell them to stop crying or get over it. That's one of the cruelest things you can do. People feel what they feel, and who are you to tell them what to do or how to feel? If they are grieving, let them grieve.

As an example, during the brief period I became depressed following the rejection of a position up north, I phoned someone in my circle of life for comfort and understanding. She has never experienced a layoff, so she could not and did not understand the enormity of emotional damage I was feeling. "Stop crying," she said. Because I was hysterical at the time, I told her, "Don't tell me to stop crying, I have to get this out!"

Oh—another thing.

Pay Attention.

During a layoff, almost the only thing the person looking for work can think is, "When is this going to end?" Nine chances out of ten, they are doing everything in their power to find work of any type. They probably aren't sleeping well, eating well, or feeling well, for that matter. There may come a time during this layoff when they may become forgetful.

"Someone under this kind of pressure is bound to occasionally say the wrong thing, do the wrong thing, wear the wrong thing, think and feel wrong thoughts and emotions," Ramin explained. "While they may outwardly look the same, inside God is doing some amazing reconstruction, and it hurts. Hurting people often times hurt people without meaning to, and sometimes without realizing they've done so.

"If your loved one comes to realizes they accidentally offended you or anyone else, please forgive them quickly, graciously, and with as much compassion and understanding as possible. You have to know under normal circumstances, they would never intentionally harm you or others."

Finally, it would be a grave mistake to tell your loved one that you "know how they feel," when both of you know that's not true. Even if you are just trying to help, it would be better to say, "I don't know what to say" or "I'm feeling very useless—tell me what you need or how I can help you. Talk as long as you want—I am here for you."

Never Underestimate the Value of Emotional Support

> *Praise be to the God and Father of our Lord Jesus Christ, the Father of compassion and the God of all comfort, who comforts us in all our troubles, so that we can comfort those in any trouble with the comfort we ourselves have received from God. (2 Corinthians 1:3-4)*

Providing emotional support is almost as important as providing financial support, at least in my opinion. Yes, we need money to pay our bills and living expenses, but we also need to know that people around us love us, support us, believe in us, and respect us, especially during a layoff. Egos can be fragile and misplaced identities are lost and found; it is a very unsettling time for all.

As an example, one afternoon during my first layoff experience, soon after my unemployment benefits stopped, I was at my brother's house, talking on the phone with the benefits counselor. Pat was upstairs in his office working and was walking down the stairs at the exact moment I put down the receiver upon hearing that my unemployment benefits would not be extended.

It must have been the look on my face that led him to ask what was wrong, and immediately it was like a dam had burst. I simply. Could not. Take it. Any longer. Poor Pat, I could tell it broke his heart to see me under such pressure. Until you've been through it, you just don't know what it's like.

"Mary," he said, holding me and letting me wail into his chest. "I am not going to let anything happen to you and Emilie. You are going to be fine." I will never forget that moment, as long as I live, because it was definitely what I needed to hear, and more important, believe.

It would be wise for you to make a mental note of your loved one's moods, how often periods of extreme sadness occur, and how long they last. A visit to the family doctor for symptoms of depression may be in order. Trust me when I say that after weeks turn into months, it can be difficult at best to maintain a positive attitude, even if you have strong faith.

If it is your husband or wife who is without a job, how you treat your spouse will make or break them during this time. Take whatever they say with a grain of salt, and understand that everyone says things they don't mean under severe pressure and duress.

"It is important to find out what the spouse needs to feel supported, and to find friends or a counselor to talk through the worries that may feel like a guilt trip to the person laid off," said David T. Moore David T. Moore, of Moore on Life Ministries.

"Too many questions about the job search can feel like a drilling and create more insecurity, ego-wise. Getting friends to call the spouse and encourage them is important, not just letting all the support come from you. Let them know that you support them, and mentally preparing for any scenario (moving, reduced salary, maybe needing to get a job yourself). Taking these steps will help you react in a more objective way to the brainstorming being done by the laid off spouse. Remember that God is not going to bring on or allow more than you can handle. Cleaning out junk can prepare you for a move, as well as create a bustle in the home that feels good, like something is happening and there are going to be changes, as moving beyond this time. Try new recipes and eat dinner by candlelight. Give everyone something to look forward to at the end of the long day," she added.

Practical Ways to Help

If you (as the family member or friend) need something done and don't have time to do it yourself, ask your loved one if they will do it for you, in exchange for whatever financial assistance you can provide. Not only will you get your chores done, you will be helping your loved one out financially *and* give them a sense of dignity and self-respect, so they aren't just standing there with their hands out.

Other ways that you could help someone out without handing them money directly would be to pay for a newspaper subscription, Internet service each month, one or more of their utilities, give them prepaid long distance phone cards for use when calling about a job or faxing a resume, or lend them your gas card. Offer to pay for computer paper, ink cartridges, or Xeroxing and faxing charges. If this individual needs medication on a regular basis, offer to pay for it.

The Best Way to Give or Loan Money

> *One man gives freely, yet gains even more; another withholds unduly, but comes to poverty. A generous man will prosper; he who refreshes others will himself be refreshed. (Proverbs 11:24-25)*

When giving money or paying bills for your loved one, do so graciously without much fanfare. The best thing to do is send them checks in the mail—without being asked to do so. Trust me, they need it. In my own experiences, I have received checks, cash, and had certain bills paid each month. No one allowed me to overdose on gratitude, they quickly change the subject when I thank them, and for that I am grateful. Please don't make the person you are helping feel indebted to you; they have enough bricks on their back to carry right now. Besides, in today's economy, you may be next in line to lose your own job. It *can* happen to you, so now is the time to treat others as you wish to be treated!

If there are several members in your family, and it is a family member who is laid off, I would recommend asking the person to provide a list of their monthly expenses to you. Then, subtract whatever unemployment benefits the person is receiving from that amount. Depending on everyone in the family's circumstances, you could split the remaining differences between everyone else and have everyone agree to send "X" amount to their loved one. If this is not possible, another idea would be to have anyone in the family who is able to help make a commitment to the layoff victim to pay "X" and/or "Y" and "Z" bills.

The most important piece of advice I can give you is this: *do not assume* that someone else is stepping up to the plate to help your loved one, because that may or may not be the case. For example, there have been times during this recent layoff experience when I had bills piling up and I was unable to pay them right away, because the funds just weren't there.

"That's your problem, you should have called someone," you might say. True, but my friend, it is easier said than done, especially when those you love have already provided help in the past.

For reasons I cannot explain or describe, I have learned to be grateful for these layoff experiences, because I am learning so much. I can feel God working in me, and although I have no clue why I have to go through losing my job again, I know there is a good reason.

> *He who is kind to the poor lends to the Lord, and He will reward him for what he has done. (Proverbs 19:17)*

> *And do not forget to do good and to share with others, for with such sacrifices God is pleased. (Hebrews 13:16)*

It's Okay to Have It, Just Don't *Flaunt* It

Now is not the time to flaunt your good fortune or even that you still have a job. You may be thinking, "I would never do that," and for the sake of your loved one, I hope you don't. During my first layoff experience, I was on the receiving end of this sort of behavior from someone I called "friend" and let me tell you, it was extremely hurtful.

One day a few weeks ago, I went shopping with someone. Unlike many times in the past, this experience was different. While this individual strolled up and down the aisles filling their cart, my cart was empty, except for a $7.48 ink cartridge that I was fighting with myself over, trying to give myself permission to buy it. "Need" versus "want," mind you.

The ink cartridge for my printer had run out, and I needed a new one. Or did I? Meantime, my loved one had absolutely no idea in the world how I felt that day. If they had, not only would they have felt terribly guilty and ashamed, they would have either bought me everything in sight or suggested we leave and they would return without me. This person kept asking if I saw anything I wanted. Of *course* I saw things I wanted! Again, it all boils down to determining "want" versus "need." Thankfully, my dilemma over whether to allow myself to spend $7.48 on an ink cartridge was solved, because my loved one bought it for me. I both wanted and needed it.

God knows your heart, and He also knows your motives. You can run but you cannot hide, and I feel sorry for anyone who thinks they can pull a fast one on Him. Don't give in order to hold something over your loved one's head, and don't think because you have given, that you can somehow control that person. Go out of your way to love your layoff victim. Remind your loved one how much he or she is loved.

I am not suggesting that you provide financial assistance to get something back later on in life, from them or anyone else. That would be a mistake. After all, the Lord looks at the heart of man, according to 1 Samuel 16:7.

The bottom line is, give what you can, when you can, without asking. If possible, make a commitment to the person as to exactly what you can and cannot do each month, because they need to make appropriate arrangements to pay their expenses and continue through life until the next job becomes a reality.

> *For we must all appear before the judgment seat of Christ, that each one may receive what is due him for the things done while in the body, whether good or bad. (2 Corinthians 5:10)*

Are *You* a "Survivor"?

With all of the reality-based television programming clogging up our minds today, I would love to see someone do a similar program on the daily life of a layoff victim. Would you be capable of surviving what your loved one is going through? Care to see what it's like?

I suspect you're not going to like this challenge, but I'm giving it to you all the same. Agreeing to give it a try by signing a contract and giving it to your loved one would be beneficial not only to him or her, but to you, as well. Upon completion of this scientific experiment, your loved one will know that you cared enough to undergo a bit of discomfort for their sake, and you will have a better understanding of what it feels like to be without a job.

The idea is simple, but as with most tests, it may prove more difficult than you can imagine. I challenge you to refuse to buy the things that you want for a thirty-day period. I'm talking no more nail polish, Starbucks, fishing lures, candy bars or even going to the movies. I'm talking refusing to buy any of your kids whatever silly thing they "have to have." After all, laid-off parents can't afford to give their kids anything but the basic necessities, so if you're going to do this, then do it. Instead, carry a small notepad with you at all times, documenting the items or events on the left and next to them, on the right side, the cost of such item or event. I mean it—not even a pack of gum!

At the end of the thirty-day period, have a look at all of the things you *thought* you had to have to be happy or have a good day, and then tally up the totals of all items listed. You will be amazed that you managed to live without these things, and astonished at the amount of money you saved by denying yourself. Then, the crème-de-la-crème of the lesson: You write a check for that amount and give it to the unemployed individual in your life.

I triple-dog dare you to try this out. Remember that if you do, while you may think it is difficult, you have the luxury of knowing that it is all a game. For your loved one, it is anything but a game—it's life, and there is no way of knowing how long it will last.

You will see first-hand, what you can and cannot live without. You will have a momentary snapshot of how immensely difficult it can be to live in a materialistic world saturated with clever advertising designed to make you feel less than a worthy human being if you don't buy or use their products.

> *Naked a man comes from his mother's womb, and as he comes, so he departs. He takes nothing from his labor that he can carry in his hand. (Ecclesiastes 5:15)*

> *But godliness with contentment is great gain. For we brought nothing into the world, and we can take nothing out of it. But if we have food and*

> *clothing, we will be content with that. People who want to get rich fall into temptation and a trap and into many foolish and harmful desires that plunge men into ruin and destruction. For the love of money is the root of all kinds of evil. (1 Timothy 6:6-10)*

> *Do not store up for yourselves treasures on Earth, where moth and rust destroy, and where thieves break in and steal. But store up for yourself treasures in Heaven, where moth and rust do not destroy, and where thieves do not break in and steal. For where your treasure is, there your heart will be also. (Matthew 6:19-21)*

Please note in the text of the contract that nothing is mentioned about writing a check out for the total amount of money you would have normally spent on yourself and your family. I think it would be such a nice surprise if you did this on your own. Either way, just signing this contract, giving it to your loved one and then sticking to the terms of it for a thirty-day period, will mean more to them than you will ever know.

But remember: God is watching everything you say and do, and you can run but you sure can't hide! If you agree to do this—then do it!

What's this? You don't *want* to do it? You don't *think* you can do it? Imagine how your loved one feels, given that he or she has no choice in the matter and no end in sight.

Point taken?

Blessed is the man who perseveres under trial, because when he has stood the test, he will receive the crown of life that God has promised to those who love Him. (James 1:12)

He who gives to the poor will lack nothing, but he who closes his eyes to them receives many curses. (Proverbs 28:27)

Suppose a brother or sister is without clothes and daily food. If one of you says to him, Go, I wish you well; keep warm and well fed, but does nothing about his physical needs, what good is it? (James 2:15-16)

If anyone has material possessions and sees his brother in need but has not pity on him, how can the love of God be in him? (1 John 3:17)

He who oppresses the poor shows contempt for their Maker, but whoever is kind to the needy honors God. (Proverbs 14:31)

Help for the Laid Off

Hardship Contract

I, _____, agree not to buy anything I want for the next thirty days, including things my children and/or spouse want. I also agree not to attend any social event or anything that costs money, unless it is required of me for my job. I agree to write down a list of everything I want to spend money on during this time but do not, including the price of the item or social event. I do this out of love for _____, to help gain a better understanding of what he/she is going through.

Signed this _____ day of _____, _____.

_____
Name

CHAPTER NINE

You're in the Promised Land—Now What?

Whatever you do, work at it with all your heart, as working for the Lord, not for men, since you know that you will receive an inheritance from the Lord as a reward. It is the Lord Christ you are serving.
Colossians 3:23-24

Unless God has seen fit to bless you with the right job while reading this book, chances are you are still without work and are dreaming of reaching the "land' (job) God has promised you. It is coming, I promise!

Once God delivers you from this desert season of your life, there are things He wants you to remember, know and do with what you've learned, while working in your new position. Here is what He brought to my mind to share with you, for all of us to follow:

1. Don't ever forget how God provided for all of your needs during your layoff. The experience was undoubtedly uncomfortable, but chances are good that

Help for the Laid Off

you had food to eat, clothes to wear, and a roof over your head. These are the absolute, bottom-line necessities.

2. God wants you to share with everyone you can what you learned from being without work. If God became real to you for the first time in your life, tell them! Did you, like me during my first layoff, learn that all of His promises really *are* true? Share this with others!

3. Once you are gainfully employed, God will most likely send people into your life, who are without work or who become unemployed during the course of your relationship with them. I can think of no better way to honor God than to minister to these people by encouraging them, offering much-needed compassion, and helping them in any way that you can—including financially.

4. Don't make the same mistake as King Nebuchadnezzar in the Old Testament. The book of Daniel tells the story of how pride got the best of the king, and he went from living in a kingdom to living in a field like a wild animal, because he never acknowledged God as the sovereign Most High.

> *All this happened to King Nebuchadnezzar. Twelve months later, as the king was walking on the roof of the royal palace of Babylon, he said, Is this not the great Babylon I have built as the royal residence, by my mighty power and for the glory of my majesty? The words were still on his lips when a voice came from Heaven, This is what is decreed for you, King Nebuchadnezzar: Your royal authority has been taken from you. You will be driven away from people and will live with the wild animals;*

> *you will eat grass like cattle. Seven times will pass by for you until you acknowledge that the Most High is sovereign over the kingdoms of men and gives them to anyone He wishes. Immediately what had been said about Nebuchadnezzar was fulfilled. He was driven away from people and ate grass like cattle. His body was drenched with dew of Heaven until his hair grew like the feathers of an eagle and his nails like the claws of a bird. (Daniel 4:28-33)*

5. Based on personal experience after my first layoff, which lasted two years, I highly recommend that you not lose your mind when you get your first few paychecks. By this, I mean that after having gone for so long without a real paycheck of your own, it is very, very easy and tempting to buy everything in sight.

You and your family have gone through a lot during your layoff, and you have been forced to deny yourself so many things that most of us take for granted; things like being able to go to the movies, buy CDs or DVDs, buy clothes, books, even fresh catfish instead of canned tuna at three cans for a dollar.

It is scary how easily you can get into debt after having gone without for so long. You never know what tomorrow will bring, as I quickly learned after a used car I bought for my then sixteen-year-old daughter ended up costing so much money in car repairs that I am still paying on that credit card, seven years later!

> *Go to the ant, you sluggard; consider its ways and be wise! It has no commander, no overseer*

or ruler, yet it stores its provisions in summer and gathers its food at harvest. (Proverbs 6:6-8)

In the house of the wise are stores of choice food and oil, But a foolish man devours all he has. (Proverbs 21:20)

Do not be a man who strikes his hand in pledge or puts up security for debts; If you lack the means to pay, your very bed will be snatched from under you. (Proverbs 22:26-27)

6. If the job God has brought you pays less than what you were making, you may consider humbling yourself and taking it anyway. So many times, we will never know why God does what He does. That's why He is God, and we are not. It could be that there is someone at this company who needs to teach you something, or you need to teach them something or minister to them in some way. A job is more than a paycheck.

As you have probably learned by now, money is not everything, and it doesn't buy happiness. Look at everything you have learned to get along without, during your layoff! Perhaps the job God knows is best for you may not pay the most in terms of money but will be closer to home, allow you more time with your family, or be the ignition switch to the career change of your dreams!

Do not wear yourself out to get rich; have the wisdom to show restraint. (Proverbs 23:4)

You're in the Promised Land—Now What?

It could be that God wants to test your level of trust and obedience to Him, to make sure all pride has, like Elvis, left the building. You never know, mi amigo. If you pass Layoff 101, God's real blessing in the way of the best job you could ever imagine, may be just around the corner (as it was for me after my first layoff ended).

Trust and obey, it's the only way.

7. Remember to keep your eyes on God and do not forget where you came from. Don't let your new job become an idol in your life. It is understandable when after being without work for so long, a person may want to be there at 4 a.m. when the world is still asleep, staying until late in the evening because he or she is so thrilled and grateful to be working. But don't do it. Enjoy your job, work to live but don't live to work!

> *A man can do nothing better than to eat and drink and find satisfaction in his work. This too, I see, is from the hand of God, for without Him who can eat or find enjoyment? To the man who pleases Him, God gives wisdom, knowledge and happiness, but to the sinner he gives the task of gathering and storing up wealth to hand it over to the one who pleases God. (Ecclesiastes 2:24-26)*

8. Whatever your job is, whether you like it, whether it pays enough, whether you get along with everyone—work like you've never worked before. Do whatever you are being paid to do, and do it with a cheerful spirit and to the best of your ability.

Help for the Laid Off

Slaves, obey your earthly masters with respect and fear, and with sincerity of heart, just as you would obey Christ. Obey them not only to win their favor when their eye is on you, but like slaves of Christ, doing the will of God from your heart. Serve wholeheartedly, as if you were serving the Lord, not men, because you know that the Lord will reward everyone for whatever good he does, whether he is slave or free. (Ephesians 6:5-8)

Chapter Ten

U.S. Pastors Speak Out on How Layoffs Affect the Church

As previously mentioned, layoffs affect everyone in some form or fashion. Even if you are not a layoff victim or do not know anyone who is laid off, you are still affected by way of the Church as a whole, as the body of Christ. If you are a Christian, you are a member of the body of Christ. And just as it is with your family members and friends, when one person suffers, we all suffer.

I spoke with the following pastors to try and get an accurate representation of how layoffs are affecting their congregations and ministries, across America:

- Pastor Charles Lyons, Ph.D., ministry coordinator, Winning Walk Ministry, Second Baptist Church in Houston, Texas
- David T. Moore, founder, Moore on Life Ministries, New Community Church in Indio, California
- James M. Jodrey, stewardship and benevolence pastor, Walk in the Word Ministry, Harvest Bible Chapel in Rolling Hills, Illinois

Help for the Laid Off

QUESTION: Has your church family and/or ministry noticed an increase in layoff victims over the past couple of years? If so, please explain.

Walk in the Word Ministries (WITW): "It is my opinion that the high-flying '90s caused many to think that 'the good times' wouldn't and couldn't end. Many in the tech and communications field who have lost their jobs are still waiting for that big paying job to drop in their lap. Others listened to Scriptures such as 2 Thessalonians 3:10, which states, 'For even when we were with you, we gave you this rule: 'If a man will not work, he shall not eat,' and took some type of work just to put food on the table.

We have definitely seen an increase in prayer requests related to job needs since September 11, 2001. I think I can safely say that the number of job/financial-related prayer requests have increased five- to seven-fold during the past two years. So much so, that we hold 'job seeker workshops' every other month for a full day. Since we placed this ministry on our website [www.walkintheword.org], I have received at least two to three inquiries via email each week, in addition to the phone calls and prayer requests.

Last year, we ministered to 150 people who were in the job search process through these workshops, and an additional sixty people who were considering a job change. In addition to conducting job-seeker workshops and career-planner workshops, we encourage job seekers to be in a small group for prayer support and networking."

Winning Walk Ministries (WWF): "We actually received an increase in two areas. On a national basis, it is true that we received a significant increase in requests for prayer, resources and counseling since September 11 [2001]. The pressure has been higher and because of the national demands, support systems that traditionally have been in place have paled in comparison to the demand. That was the initial increase that probably resulted in about a 25 percent increase in our communications, mainly through phone calls.

"The second aspect has stemmed from our gearing up to handle these calls in a more proactive approach. We have engaged in more follow-up activities and attempted more local resource coordination. That is to say we have never felt it was enough at the Winning Walk to simply touch a life and move on. We want to get resources to the individual and find a local source that they can plug into that can continue with the individual or family. We frequently connect people either with the Rapha [Christian] Counseling group or make a direct contact on their behalf with a local church.

"Locally, there was an additional element that we have had to deal with. Shortly before September 11, Houston experienced a significant flood that displaced more than a fourth of the population. At that same time, 'rightsizing' was rampant. At a time when families, single parent families, and individuals needed help most, their insurance was disappearing along with their income. We worked with that aspect and, while there was a significant outpouring from the community and organizations, it was mostly short-term processing. This is to say, trash was cleared, roads improved, the Red Cross posed for pictures, and sandwiches were passed out.

"There was a 25 percent increase in call traffic initially. However, we surged dramatically when you include the follow-up calls and contacts that we made to try and deal with these issues. Overall, we handled 45 percent more calls at years' end than we had in the preceding year that was directly attributed to this follow-up process."

QUESTION: Has the increase in layoffs affected your benevolence funds?

WITW: "Our benevolence fund experienced a 120 percent increase in expenses last year compared to 2001, much of that was due to job loss."

WWF: "We have had contact with about 4,700 people last year in this category, compared to about 1,700 the preceding year. Maintaining effective change initiative-type support systems are demanding both in staff and financially. Since 'benevolence funds' are a different area, they began being more limited. Add to this the increased level of demand that may be needed either initially at a September 11-type event and then the added financial resources that may be needed to help through the transition, and you can exhaust the resource long before the need or transition is complete. Personally, our own resources have been affected to the extent that we limit our benevolence to members who are involved in a Bible study class and have done so for at least a year."

QUESTION: What are the biggest differences in the way couples and single parents handle layoff situations?

Moore on Life (MOL): "A layoff can cause extreme stress in a marriage when it is the male that is the one laid off. Because the male usually uses his career or job as his identity, it is very important that the wife continue to support him emotionally and make him feel needed. One of the top five needs of a man is to feel esteemed by his wife anyway, and this is very important when something happens—like a layoff—that damages that.

"Single moms already have the hardest job on the planet, and a layoff makes it even harder. They are probably the sole provider, so that provision is now gone. This is where the church family should step in and provide help."

WITW: "People will refuse to seek help or godly counsel when they lose a job. This is particularly true of men. We [as men] won't seek help—certainly not counsel—and definitely not the church's help. I usually get to see these families when it is almost too late. They are a financial basket case by the time they get to benevolence.

Single moms, on the other hand, seem to be more practical and will come for help when they can't make the next rent payment. I've seen parents refuse to tell their kids what is going on when a job is lost, even teenage children who could help. That wasn't the case in 2 Kings 4:1-7. She put her sons to work to help the family out of debt. Single moms don't have time to sit back and think about their circumstances."

WWF: "Stress does have a dramatic impact on families and individuals. In our society, a tremendous measure of self-worth is derived from our work. Far more than simply the financial loss, the emotional loss is devastating.

"Consider the single parent whose principle adult interaction is from the workplace. When the job is lost, so is a significant support group or system. In most situations when the job is gone, co-workers no longer communicate or associate with the one who is leaving. As a result, a person who may still be recovering from the 'desertion' effect of a divorce feels an additional level of 'desertion' from the workplace family. The person who has been living for work is now an orphan.

"The added pressures in the home of meeting financial obligations generated during a time when 'we knew we were fixed for life,' can break a relationship. If the couple never had a budget, never had good communication, were stronger spenders than savers, they will find destructive behavior driven from the outside will be focused inside at the very ones they need the most.

"Since often people separate the fiscal issues of life from the spiritual issues, they may not even see their local church as an option for support. Additionally, many local churches do not have anything in place for this. A benevolence fund is short-term help at best, and does not address the issues of retraining, helping someone prepare a resume, helping someone who has not done an interview either before or in the last ten years, and to help integrate people into people networks that can open doors. People who have been 'happy' in their jobs frequently have had a tight sphere of friends only from the one organization. They will not be hiring.

"Finally, we must consider the multiple-issue effect. Tests and studies have been done that identified stress levels that not only have various values or levels, but they are accumulative over a year's period. Losing a job is a significant event in a person or family's life. But so is a death in the family, a divorce, and a loss of a child, or a natural disaster. Those entire events rate at about the same level. However, many people don't realize that birthdays, holidays, and weddings also rate as high emotional stressors. Psychologists know that stressors are cumulative and as a result, you may be able to snap back from a job loss, divorce or a loss such as September 11. However, you will need professional help or suffer significant trauma if you sustain a 'September 11' and lose your job and go straight into Thanksgiving and Christmas. What I described here would be very, very difficult for a believer with the Spirit of God operating within and alongside the individual. Alone, it would be devastating.

"The stressors for single parents are similar to what others face and have to deal with because they have to deal with all of the same issues that any family has to deal with. The difference is that the majority of all support systems are designed for families and couples.

"Consider a homeless shelter. If you are a wife with children, there are shelters that will take you in. If you are already alone with a child, you may get help but you are not considered 'urgent.' If you are single, you are down on the list for help. If you are a male, there may not be any help since support systems are designed to help those in need, and men are not viewed in society as the group in need.

"One advantage a woman has is that they tend to be more realistic in assessing the desperateness of a situation, which will drive them to seek help. However, they may view the situation out of proportion, and that is why the support helps can be so valuable. When you are in the midst of devastation, you desperately need perspective. Support counselors and volunteers can help with that. When you know that people love and care about you, there is a tremendous strength that comes.

"Regarding the opposites between single women and single moms, a single mom is viewed as stable, while a single woman is not. It may not be right, but it is a stereotype that has to be recognized and dealt with or you will operate as a confused victim rather than the child of God that you are.

"A single mom has support systems that are available from day care to special classes at church, through ministries and in the secular 'good-works' systems. If you are a single woman, it may not be clear that you even have a need—you are simply single, 'go get work and get on with life.' This is cold, impersonal, and fails to deal with reality.

"Numerous subtleties continue as there are tax benefits to a single parent; there are none for a single man or woman. There are special emphasis programs for single parents; there may be dating events for single women. Employers view a single mom as someone who will be with them long-term, which may be an asset in hiring. The single woman may be viewed as ready to relocate or wanting to go back to school, which will take time and sometimes money from the job.

"Single mothers can identify with many employers who are married or divorced predominantly so a natural communication begins to build. Not so, with the single woman. Worst of all in the workforce, single moms need to go home at the end of the day, need to be off for holidays, and certainly need a raise with the expenses of being a single mom. Single women have no obligations (no life) so they should stay late, work holidays, and work for minimum wage.

QUESTION: Other than the benevolence fund, what are some ways in which your church family and/or ministry helps layoff victims?

MOL: "Southwest Community Church, where I was former pastor before leaving in November [2002], offered career counseling, emergency bill paying, and food."

WITW: "We are about six months into putting programs into place to specifically help single moms, such as a car-maintenance and donation program, a home maintenance program, and individual financial counseling. Single moms have greater needs when they lose their jobs, because they don't have reserves and often times no family members to help.

"In addition to conducting job-seeker and career-planner workshops, we encourage job seekers to be in a small group for prayer support and networking. Our benevolence and stewardship ministry is very active, and we also provide spiritual and financial counseling."

WWF: "Our church offers some rather unusual but effective tools. There are classes that run in cycles of several weeks where people can get help in preparing a resume, doing an interview, networking, where to look for employment and methods and places to begin retraining. Additionally, employers often leave job announcements with the church that are placed in books that people can schedule time to review for follow-up. They can also arrange to have their resumes placed in a book that prospective employers can come and spend time reviewing for applicants."

QUESTION: Have you noticed a difference in the amounts of tithing and offering received by your church and/or ministries? If so, please explain.

MOL: "No, tithing has been steady, if not increasing."

WITW: "Although the weekly tithing went down after September 11, we met our annual need by year's end. Last year we were very cautious in our budget planning and again this year. However, God is good and faithful, as He exceeded our budgeted need last year and we are ahead of our need this year.

"In the midst of all this, we have been looking for land to relocate to for two years, as we have outgrown the facility we've been in for the last eight years. Well, God did a miracle in our midst in February. He gave us an 80-acre site located 25 miles from here, with a 265,000 square-foot building on it, provided as a gift to us from the owners of Hobby Lobby.

"I believe this speaks to the faithfulness of God, who is alive and at work in this congregation. We could have made many mistakes in the past two years, but He protected us and gave us more than we prayed for. We will run two campuses as a result of this gift.

"God promises abundance if we give abundantly. His people gave faithfully during uncertain times and when we didn't know where He was leading us. Honor God with your finances, and He will honor you" (Proverbs 3:9-10).

Author's Note
A report issued by the Barna Research Group, "Tithing Down 62 Percent in the Past Year," indicates that, "The proportion of households that tithe their income to their church—that is, give at least ten percent of their income to that ministry—has dropped by 62 percent in the past year, from 8 percent in 2001 to just 3 percent of adults during 2002."

"Born again adults, who represent 38 percent of the nation's population, also sustained a decline in generosity during the past couple of years. In 2000, 12 percent of all born again adults tithed. The percentage rose to 14 percent in 2001, but dropped to only 6 percent in 2002," the report stated.

"Different challenges have caused people to choose not to tithe. For some, the soft economy has either diminished their household income or led to concerns about their financial security," said Researcher George Barna, in the report.

Barna Research Group online, www.barna.org, May 19, 2003. 5528 Everglades, Ventura, CA 93003.

Epilogue

With great pleasure, I conclude this journey with you by sharing how God blessed me at the end of this layoff. It is now April 2009, and my life has changed dramatically since I wrote this book in 2003.

The night my mother died, I prayed, "Lord, I still love you, but this really hurts. Please give me something good in exchange for my mother's pain, suffering and death."

The words "Senior Sitters Ministry" came to me at 1:30 a.m. along with a passion to spend time with elderly people who were sick at a time when their adult children could not be with them, whether in a facility or in their home. The Lord brought to me those He wanted me to befriend during the second layoff, and continued to do so after I found employment.

In May 2004, God provided a new full-time editorial position, this time covering the healthcare industry for a magazine devoted to registered nurses. I found this so like the Lord, because He used this position to help heal emotional wounds I incurred during the loss of my mother, who passed away of medical negligence.

I quickly learned there is a nursing shortage. Although I quickly forgave all medical professionals responsible for her suffering and death, I developed a new respect for nurses that I otherwise would not have had. My mother's graduation into Heaven helped renew my passion for journalism because I was intent on interviewing the best sources for each article to provide the most accurate information possible to the magazine's subscribers.

While working for the magazine, I was given the privileged opportunity to help one of my church family's most beloved pastors by caring for his wife, who has Alzheimers. God gave me a second set of parents when He brought me into the DeLoach family. It was such a rewarding experience that when the pastor asked me if I would consider working for him full-time in this capacity, I didn't think twice about doing so, and quickly ended my career as a journalist.

Around this same time, God brought into my life John, one of the finest, kindest Christian men I've ever known. We began an old-fashioned courtship and by God's grace, our relationship bloomed beautifully and slowly over time. My mom used to say, "The longer it stews, the better it tastes," and she was right!

Shortly before the pastor and his wife relocated far away, John proposed. We were ushered into marriage by this pastor in the same chapel my mother's memorial service was held, among family and close friends.

Ironically enough, I was without a job again, and same as before, I had been applying for all types of jobs. How wonderful to know for the first time in my life, I have a husband to love and be loved by, to take care of, who is also taking care of me.

Epilogue

No one was more surprised and delighted than me to receive a publishing contract out of the blue, since this book was written six years ago.

God's infinite wisdom, timing and plans for my life never cease to amaze me.

You cannot tell me that He is not real, and that He has not been with me all this time. Dear Reader, please listen to me. God loves you, and while His plans for you are probably going to be different than His plans for me, they are equally wonderful if you trust and obey Him. God is no respecter of persons; we are all created in His image and He loves each of us the same. I am no one special, yet I am special to Him.

And so are you.

In Closing

Whoever you are, it is my most sincere, heartfelt desire that God has spoken to you through this book. If you have never accepted Jesus Christ as your Lord and Savior, I cannot end this book without extending you the chance to do so once again. It is so simple.

"God, I do believe you are real, and I do believe Jesus Christ is your Son, and that He lived and died as payment for my sins. I am sorry for everything I have ever done wrong, every sin I've ever committed. By faith, I am asking for your forgiveness, and by faith, I receive it. Please, fill me with your Holy Spirit and take control of my life. I'm tired of the train wrecks I'm creating, and I'm tired of feeling so alone and empty. I'm tired of not knowing what to do with my life or why I'm even here. All that I have, and all that I am, I give to you, in Jesus' name, Amen."

To my weary Christian brothers and sisters who believe they can't take this anymore, please don't give up on God or yourself. I know you are hurting, I know you are scared and rightfully so. But the same God who is working in my life, is also working in yours. I don't know how He does it, but you must continue to believe in and trust Him to work all things out for your good and His glory.

He's doing it right now.